PREPARING WITNESSES

4TH EDITION

PREPARING WITNESSES

4TH EDITION

DANIEL I. SMALL

A PRACTICAL GUIDE FOR
LAWYERS AND THEIR CLIENTS

Cover design by Monica Alejo/ABA Publishing.

Printed in the United States of America.

18 17 16 15 14   5 4 3 2 1

Library of Congress Cataloging-in-Publication data on file.

Discounts are available for books ordered in bulk. Special consideration is given to state bars, CLE programs, and other bar-related organizations. Inquire at Book Publishing, ABA Publishing, American Bar Association, 321 N. Clark Street, Chicago, Illinois 60654-7598.

www.ShopABA.org

Contents

About the Author

Dan Small is a partner in the Boston and Miami offices of Holland & Knight LLP. He is a member of the firm's trial, white collar, health law, education, and securities litigation practice groups. Mr. Small's practice focuses on a broad range of internal and external investigations, complex civil litigation, witness preparation, and white-collar criminal matters. Mr. Small has extensive jury trial and other litigation experience, based on ten years as a federal prosecutor and many years in private practice. He is the author of two other best-selling American Bar Association books, *Going to Trial* and *Letters for Litigators*. His books have become the foundation of successful ABA, state bar, client groups, and law firm CLE programs around the country.

Mr. Small has been involved in several high-profile cases around the country. He was lead defense attorney for former Louisiana Governor Edwin Edwards, counsel in a prominent SEC Internet fraud case, Special Counsel to the Rhode Island Ethics Commission, and Special Counsel to the Massachusetts House Ethics Committee. He was general counsel for a publicly traded health-care management firm, where he oversaw in-house legal and risk management staff, outside counsel, professional liability and other litigation, and facility, entity, and physician contracting. Mr. Small was also a Lecturer at Harvard Law School, where he taught federal litigation. He has taught trial advocacy at Harvard and at other law schools and CLE programs. Mr. Small is a frequent newspaper, television, and Internet commentator.

Acknowledgments

No trial lawyer learns in a vacuum. To whatever extent the several editions of this book contain wisdom of value, it is wisdom learned from the large number of extraordinary lawyers, clients, and others I have been privileged to work with in over 25 years as a trial lawyer. Most of the examples in the book are from real cases—some involving these individuals—but they may have been modified slightly for simplicity. My apologies to those involved for anything I may have missed or mistaken.

Any attempt to list all those to whom I owe my gratitude would be a fruitless exercise—an absurdly long list that would inevitably miss important people. However, at the risk of offending others, I do want to thank a few of those most directly involved in this book, including:

- The partners, associates, and staff at Holland & Knight, for their patience and support.
- My wife, Alix, and our children, Bailey, Schuyler, and Gabrielle, for pushing me to write and for offering the love and sacrifices that allowed me to do it.

Introduction

In recent years, this country has seen an explosion of government and private investigations, litigation, and other inquiries. With this explosion has come a great increase in the number and variety of people who have been dragged into these proceedings as witnesses—for either "informal" interviews or testimony. The result is that a large number of laypeople who have never been witnesses, and many lawyers whose practices have not previously involved witness preparation, have had to venture into this strange new world. Yet being a witness is often a significant event for the individuals involved and for the integrity of our system of justice. It demands careful attention and preparation by lawyer and client alike.

Recent scandals have shown that being called as a witness can happen to anyone: A young White House intern becomes the focus of a major criminal grand jury investigation, while everyone from the maid to her mom to the president becomes a potential witness. A stockbroker's assistant brings down a homemaking diva. Whether the witness is a young student facing a disciplinary board, a businessperson facing the Securities and Exchange Commission, a health-care provider facing a jury, or any other ordinary person in this very extraordinary process, it can be a bizarre and frightening experience. In an ideal world, any inquiry ought to be an open, shared search for the truth. In reality, we operate in an adversarial system in which people get wrapped up in their "side." As a result, they lose perspective and "see what they want to see," and they do not simply ask questions to find out the facts.

First and foremost, the job of a witness is to tell the truth. Alas, it sounds simple, but it is not. The job of a witness is to keep perspective: not on some cosmic truth, but simply on the truth as they knew it then, and remember it now. This is neither an easy nor a natural assignment: to do it right takes hard work. The critical importance of preparation regarding the process of *how* to be a witness—not just reviewing the facts—is based on the fundamental difference between communicating in a normal conversation and communicating in a precise and unnatural question-and-answer format.

The purpose of this book is to help lawyers improve their witness preparation skills. Parts of it are written in the "voice" of speaking to a client, because learning *how* to best communicate these ideas is often as important as the ideas themselves. Going through the general concepts, focusing on a series of clear and simple rules, then discussing how to adapt those rules to different situations can assist you in that preparation effort. The CD-ROM that accompanies this book contains all the appendix material, including memoranda outlining these rules (see corresponding filenames in the table of contents).

At times, the writing speaks directly to the witness; this is to give lawyers the option of sharing this book with clients. We all learn best by gathering information and understanding from more than one source and in more than one way. Think about how you learned a foreign language or other challenging subject in school: you listened to your teacher, read from a book, and practiced. No one would learn as well by doing only one of those three tasks.

The same principles apply to learning this strange new language. This book is not legal advice. It is simply intended to be *another* source of learning, to complement what clients hear from counsel and absorb from practice. Properly used, it should make the time a lawyer and client spend together more productive and more efficient.

The message to both lawyer and client is: Don't be intimidated. You can learn this new "language" (actually, it is not so much a language as a communications process). Many people who go through the whole process find themselves surprised at what an intense, interesting learning experience it turns out to be. However, it will be very difficult unless you and your client understand one simple fact: This is not a conversation. It is, as they say in *The Wizard of Oz*, "a horse of a different color."

Note

There are many different witness situations, from government interviews to formal jury trials, and everything in between. Each is different in various ways, and yet all are founded in surprisingly common themes, and all raise the same fundamental preparation issues. As a compromise to writing a book aimed at this full range of situations, I have focused most often on the middle of this range: the deposition. Later chapters address some of the differences, but what is far more striking are the similarities. *All* witness situations require this extraordinary preparation process, with the same basic concepts and rules.

Chapter 1

"Please Raise Your Right Hand . . ."

- An ordinary person walks into a room full of strangers.
- Someone with an odd-looking machine is taking down every word.
- A stranger is waiting to ask difficult questions and pick apart the answers.
- The person is told to raise their right hand and swear under oath.

As Dorothy exclaimed upon entering the bizarre Land of Oz: "Oh, Toto, I've a feeling we're not in Kansas anymore!"

When someone is called as a witness in any kind of legal matter, it is usually a new and disturbing experience. Still, too few people—and too few lawyers—understand just how completely new and different it really is. *This is not a conversation*: it doesn't look like one or feel like one, so no one should expect it to *be* like one. Communicating effectively in a question-and-answer format is an extraordinarily unnatural and difficult process. A witness must learn a new and strange language and a discipline that is very different than anything we use in our everyday lives.

I was fortunate enough to begin to learn this lesson early in my legal career. Just out of law school and still trying to find my way around the labyrinthine hallways of the Department of Justice in Washington, I was assigned to the team prosecuting Bert Lance, the former U.S. budget director and lifelong friend of then-president Jimmy Carter, in his home town of Atlanta, Georgia. It was an opportunity for a new lawyer to learn many lessons. The lesson for this purpose came with the testimony of President Carter's mother, "Miss Lillian."

1

The defense had made a strategic error (one of their few in a well-tried case). They had presented the judge with a list of about 50 people they intended to call as character witnesses for Lance. Character testimony has largely faded from trial practice today, but the idea was fairly simple: witnesses who knew the defendant and his reputation in the community were called to testify, in essence to say, "Bert's a good guy, and he would not have done this terrible thing." Since it has questionable value in this day and age, it can be severely restricted under federal law. The judge, with visions of weeks of testimony from this absurdly long list, used his authority to do just that: the defense could ask character witnesses only a handful of narrow, legalistic questions.

The defense went forward and called a few of these witnesses, including Miss Lillian. Knowing that the questions would be mumbo jumbo to someone with no legal experience, preparation was essential, and relatively easy: "Miss Lillian, the judge has limited us to these few crazy legal questions. Here they are. I don't understand them any more than you do, so let's talk through them carefully. But if at any point you're stuck, just talk about Bert. Tell us why you think he's such a good, honest person, and give us a few examples that make you believe in him!"

What could the prosecution have done? Tried to interrupt the sainted elderly mother of the sitting president in her beloved home state? That would have been an even better show for the defense than the testimony itself. No, we would have sat there and tried to act as if we didn't care, while she talked on, in her own words. But whether it was due to lack of time or opportunity, or to some other reason, Miss Lillian apparently had not been prepared. She came into the courtroom looking frail, bewildered, and out of place, and it never got much better. She was clearly put off by the legalistic questions, and gave short, unclear answers. Then, all of a sudden, the defense was out of questions and had to sit down, having gotten nothing of substance from her. Their only hope for this witness was that the prosecution would open things up on cross-examination.

However, the cross was handled by a veteran prosecutor, Marvin Loewy, who had no intention of opening anything up, but who, in his own way, had prepared the witness better than the defense had. He had made sure to be out in the hallway when Miss Lillian arrived and had greeted her with all his considerable charm. In the courtroom, when he rose for cross-examination, he had that same smile. Miss Lillian saw a friend, and brightened in response. Loewy reminded her that they had met, she sweetly agreed, and then he thanked her for coming, and sat down. It was over. As she left the courtroom after these strange proceedings, Miss Lillian looked over at Lance and said, "I wish it could have been longer."

I assume that if you had sat on the front porch with Miss Lillian over a glass of iced tea and asked her to tell you about Bert Lance, it *would* have been longer. She would have had lots to say: high praise, heartwarming stories, and much more. Instead, the questions were asked in a strange environment, with an artificial formality and an unnatural language. Without adequate preparation, this potentially ideal witness was lost. It was not a question of substance: she presumably had relevant testimony. Rather, it was a problem of process: she had not been prepared to communicate in this strange new world.

In every walk of life, at every level of education, profession, or experience, we are *all* just like Miss Lillian. We know what we know (or think we do), but if we cannot communicate it effectively, we are lost. Fortunately, it is possible for anyone to learn to communicate in this question-and-answer language. However, it takes time, effort, and the assistance of a trained "guide."

Preparation is not something to be embarrassed or defensive about. Giving testimony or a statement of any kind is an important and difficult process. You won't be doing your job if you do not prepare your witness extensively. More importantly, a witness who does not take the process seriously enough to prepare carefully is not doing his or her job either.

It is critical for witnesses to understand that good preparation is not some kind of improper cover-up. It is not tantamount to making up a story or having someone tell them what to say. On the contrary, the point is to make the witness's statement *more* truthful, by helping him or her to be more thoughtful, careful, and precise. There is no magic to preparation, no magic wand that you, as a lawyer, can wave to turn your client into "Superwitness." All you can do is work together to try to develop some of the understanding and discipline that will ultimately make your client's experience as a witness much easier and more successful.

Chapter 2

Why Tell the Truth?

Why tell the truth? It sounds like a simple question for any witness, but it isn't. We all know from our daily lives that there are times when telling the truth can be a difficult path: it can be awkward, embarrassing, offensive, hurtful, even just plain wrong. We understand a world where telling "white lies" can be the best thing to do, for ourselves, and sometimes *for others*. So why tell the truth so strictly when it could cause even greater harm, in a witness environment? There are four basic reasons:

1. Lying is wrong.
2. Lying is a crime.
3. Lying is hard.
4. Lying is confusing.

1. Lying Is Wrong

To an oversimplified question, here is an oversimplified answer: lying is wrong, so don't do it. But it's true. When you raise your right hand and swear under oath to tell the truth, you put yourself out there for all to see. Betraying that oath betrays the court, the judge, the jury, and our system of justice. But most of all, it betrays you. It diminishes you and all that you stand for, and many times—not always—that diminishment becomes apparent for all to see.

2. Lying Is a Crime

Not telling the truth is not only a moral problem: it can also be a serious crime. Just for example, federal law criminalizes a wide range of false statements by a witness, including:

- False statements, 18 U.S.C. § 1001
  § 1001 makes almost any false statement to any part of the federal government—oral or written, formal or informal—a serious crime, carrying a maximum penalty of five years in prison.
- Perjury generally, 18 U.S.C. § 1621
  § 1621 makes a wide range of sworn testimony, declarations, certifications, or statements subject to criminal penalties if the declarant makes material false statements. Penalties include a maximum of five years in prison.
- False declarations before a grand jury or court, 18 U.S.C. § 1623
  § 1623 covers false statements "in any proceeding before or ancillary to any court or grand jury of the United States." This section includes a provision allowing conviction in some circumstances where the defendant "made irreconcilably contradictory declarations." Penalties again include five years in prison.

There are a number of other—sometimes overlapping—statutes covering particular proceedings, agencies, and so on. In addition, most states also have perjury and false statement statutes. Federal and state laws also prohibit suborning perjury: procuring or inducing someone to commit perjury.

3. Lying Is Hard

Witnesses should understand, to be blunt about it, that they are not as good at lying as they think they are. That's because they are used to getting away with it relatively easily. In normal conversations, certain kinds of social white lies are generally accepted or ignored. Even more serious lying is rarely directly challenged, and never with the kind of intensity and expertise you will experience if you try it as a witness. In this environment, even innocent or unintended false statements will often be pursued vigorously and repeatedly. You can't say, "Oh, never mind," or change the subject, or try any of the other myriad ways in which we seek to disguise a white lie. There's no place to hide, and inexorably, the lie may be tripped up and exposed. There is some truth in the words of the famous judge and legal scholar John Wigmore from over 100 years ago that "[cross-examination] is beyond any doubt the greatest legal engine ever invented for the discovery of truth."

4. Lying Is Confusing

It should be easy, right? Make up a story, then just follow the script. It's not, in part, because from a very young age we know the difference. Most young children love to be read to. But somewhere along the way, they make an amazing discovery: they can read themselves! From that time forward, they generally view being read to as demeaning. It's a traumatic moment for many parents. But we all know that people have a different reading voice than speaking voice, and with a few exceptions (poetry readings, etc.), we don't want to be read to.

Actors and actresses spend years of learning and practice before they can sound natural reading from a script—whether it's printed on paper or memorized in their head. It's quite a talent: night after night of performing the same play, take after take of filming a carefully scripted movie scene, and yet the actor sounds as natural and normal as if you were old friends chatting. Do *not* labor under the illusion that this is easy, or that you can do it, too. Juries and judges are, collectively, pretty good at spotting a phony, and at knowing when they're being read to from a script. And they don't like it.

There are other perils of memorizing a false story, including the following traps:

- *Memory Trap*: The longer and more complex the story, the harder it is to remember. Moreover, once our memory on one point becomes unstable, it can become like a domino that causes the whole story to collapse. Follow the wisdom of Mark Twain, who supposedly said:

Always tell the truth.

It makes it easier to remember,

What you said the first time.

- *Anxiety Trap*: Being a witness is nerve-racking in itself. So is lying, for all but pathological liars. Put the two together, and it can be a recipe for disaster.

- *Off-Script Trap*: Another danger of a script is what happens when either questioner or witness gets into something that wasn't included in the original script. Is what the witness says consistent or logical, and how does the witness get back "on script"? Don't risk it: stay with the truth.

Real witness preparation is an intensive and challenging process. However, it must begin and end with one fundamental principle: Always tell the truth. The witness must be clear and comfortable in the belief that at no time is the lawyer telling him or her what to say, other than to say the truth. We may discuss the hows and whys and words, but on the basic point there can be no confusion.

The need to tell the truth, though, does not lessen the need to prepare. On the contrary, it heightens it. To quote a very different author, Oscar Wilde, "The pure and simple truth is rarely pure and never simple." The goal of good preparation is to get to the truth, and bring it out effectively in this difficult environment. Truth is often the first casualty of poor preparation.

Chapter 3

The Gaps

Why is being a witness so difficult and so different from any other experience? The witness is the same person who explained the same facts—or other equally complex or difficult issues—to family, friends, and colleagues just yesterday. It sounded fine then. Why is this so different?

Three simple circumstances create surprising and enormous gaps between a witness's real world experiences and expectations, and those in this very strange and unnatural world of being a witness. The circumstances are easily stated, but their impact is profound. All three swirl around in dizzying fashion and ultimately collide to create a world that is foreign and unnerving even for the most intelligent and articulate witness—perhaps *especially* for the most intelligent and articulate witness.

The three simple circumstances are as follows:

- A court reporter is taking down every word as it is spoken;
- A lawyer is prepared with questions and follow-up techniques; and
- An officer is administering an oath, chiseling in stone words spoken in haste, so that they may be picked apart at leisure.

Each of these extraordinary circumstances is far beyond an ordinary person's experience. Put together, they form the basis for a series of critical gaps:

1. The Perception Gap
2. The Audience Gap
3. The Conversation Gap

4. The Control Gap

To prepare a witness, a lawyer must first define, understand, and bridge each gap, and then help the witness to do so. Each one of these gaps will be discussed in turn in the next four chapters.

Chapter 4

The Perception Gap

Defining the Perception Gap

The Witness: "The lawyer wants me to toe the company line."
The Lawyer: "I want to help the witness tell the truth."

Understanding the Perception Gap

There is, for a surprising and disturbing percentage of witnesses, an extraordinary perception gap between what the lawyer assumes he or she is asking from the witness and what the witness assumes the lawyer is seeking. One small example is telling. As part of my work with witnesses, I frequently get called in by clients around the country to prepare executives or others for depositions or other witness situations—often working with existing trial, corporate, or personal counsel. One time, several years ago, I walked into the conference room where counsel and the witness were waiting, and started to introduce myself to the witness.

She interrupted me and said, "I know who you are. You're the guy who's come to tell me what to say!" I responded, "If that's your understanding, then that guy is going to walk out the door, and I'll come back in as a different guy: one who wants only the truth." I walked out, waited five minutes, then returned, introducing myself as "the guy who's come to help you tell the truth."

Where does this perception gap come from? Most lawyers think of themselves as ethical professionals, there to give advice and help guide witnesses through this process. We're there to have an open and honest dialogue, to help witnesses understand—and tell—the truth. However, the sad reality is that most witnesses do not develop their perceptions of lawyers—particularly trial lawyers—in this way. Most witnesses develop their perceptions of lawyers in very different contexts: from TV, where unethical and devious characters get the best ratings; from the Internet, where stories of outrageous conduct by lawyers abound; and from friends and family, where tales of sleazy lawyers are far more interesting to tell, and thus far more frequently repeated, than tales of ordinary professionals acting appropriately.

So it should come as no surprise that so many witnesses assume that lawyers are there not to get at the truth but rather "to tell them what to say," to make them "toe the company line," to make sure everyone's "singing from the same song sheet," or just to tell whatever story is most likely to help win the case. Counsel should be up-front with the witness about these common negative perceptions. We all recognize the perception; now let's move forward together toward reality, recognizing that the two are often very different.

Bridging the Perception Gap

There is an old story from the late Speaker of the House Thomas "Tip" O'Neill. In his first congressional election, he campaigned all over his hometown, and worked hard, but he found out that his next-door neighbor, an elderly woman, had said she would not vote for him. He went to her house and said, "Mrs. Finley, you've known me all my life: I shoveled your driveway, mowed your lawn, delivered your paper, beginning when I was 10 years old. Why aren't you going to vote for me?"

"Tommy," she answered, "you never asked me."

Don't make that mistake. Ask your witness for the truth—not as an off-hand comment or an assumption. Ask for the truth

- early,
- clearly,
- humbly,

- passionately, and
- *repeatedly.*

Now, as a stranger, you have asked witnesses for the truth. Do they understand that you want *all* of it, not just the easy stuff? Encourage the client
to talk about sometimes difficult matters. Questioning in different types
of legal proceedings can often reach into areas that the witness views as
private, sensitive, embarrassing, or even incriminating. As a lawyer, you
cannot effectively represent your clients as witnesses if they are not fully
candid and forthcoming. As a person, you must understand that you are
asking people to say things and admit things that they may not have admit-
ted before, sometimes even to themselves. This can be a long, hard process
that must be handled with patience and feeling.

Lawyer and witness must work together to close the perception gap.

Chapter 5

The Audience Gap

Defining the Audience Gap

The Witness: "Why doesn't he understand?"
The Lawyer: "Because he's not listening!"

Understanding the Audience Gap

"Come have a seat at the table!"
"Come talk with us!"
We are social animals, and we treasure invitations to join others.

- Your spouse or relative invites you for a meal;
- Your friend invites you for a drink;
- Your coworker invites you for a meeting.

From a very young age, we learn—and enjoy—being social. We respond to and interact with those at the table. Maybe they'll agree with us and maybe they won't, but we know they will listen. We know who we are talking to—our audience is clear and is right there in front of us. Our mission is to communicate with them, to understand them, and to help them understand us.

But what if the table we are invited to is the witness table—a deposition, a hearing, or whatever? The most common and fundamental mistake many witnesses make is not understanding who the real audience is, and that the person asking the questions is often *not* the principal audience. After a lifetime of socializing with people, of listening and responding to whoever is talking to them, they assume that they're having a conversation with the questioner. But this is *not* a conversation, and in most instances, the real audience is *not* the questioner.

What a bizarre gap for a normal, sociable person—the person you are talking to is not the audience. Stranger still, in a deposition or some other witness settings, you may be talking—through the court reporter—to the real audience that is not even in the room. Indeed, we may not even know yet who he or she is: some yet-to-be-determined juror, judge, arbitrator, or other finder of fact. "Madam Witness, you are talking to a ghost!"

This audience gap is not the witness's fault; it is the lawyer's fault for not understanding how profound this misunderstanding can be, and for not making it clear in preparation. This gap is truly a wide one: it goes against all our upbringing, our socialization, our normal interactions. The idea that the person asking the questions may *not* be the person(s) the answers are directed to is hard to understand and deal with.

Bridging the Audience Gap

Explain *why* the questioner is not the audience: The questioner is often a paid advocate, hired to win, and unmovable from that advocacy no matter how personable and persuasive the witness may be. It's not a reflection on the witness; it's just the way things work. Fill in the gap from both sides. First, understand who the audience really *is*. Is it Juror #6, or a judge, or an arbitrator, or others? Who are they, what are they like, and what are they looking for? Second, discuss how the questioner can take advantage of this gap in many ways, including by playing the following roles:

- *The Friend*: The questioner pretends to be the witness's friend, to try to get the witness to tell him more, and tell him what he wants to hear, or at least to try to bend things his way, and avoid or minimize any disagreements. But he is not your friend. Don't lose focus.

- *The Interpreter*: Trying to be "helpful," the questioner puts the witness's testimony in his own words: "So, what you're really saying is . . ."; "Let me see if I can sum this up . . ."; "Then, wouldn't you agree that . . ."; and more. This is your testimony, not his. Don't let anyone put words in your mouth.

- *The Jerk*: We've all met him—or her—the infuriating person who offends you and goads you into an argument. But here, the questioner knows that if the witness is busy arguing with him, then the witness is forgetting about—and likely making a poor impression with—the real audience. Don't engage with the questioner. He's not the audience.

- *The Cynic*: How frustrating it can be to be at the table with someone who just won't agree with you, no matter what you say. That frustration can cause you to go overboard in making your point, or to just shut down and not bother. But the questioner is not the audience; the witness is not going to change the questioner's mind (or at least the questioner will never admit to that happening). If the witness reacts to the questioner as cynic, in any of the normal ways, it will be much harder for the witness to communicate with the *real* audience, as the questioner knows.

An officer administers an oath, chiseling the witness's words in stone so that they can be examined and picked apart at leisure. This creates an unnatural environment of extraordinary narrowness and precision. Witnesses must speak the language of question-and-answer, filled with care and caution they are not used to in normal environments. Just as important, they must speak in the *rhythm* of question-and-answer: a slow, deliberate progression of question, pause, answer, stop—the same rhythm, repeated over and over like a series of one-act plays. It is an unnatural pace—but it is an unnatural environment.

Chapter 6

The Conversation Gap

Defining the Conversation Gap

The Witness: "I'll just go talk to them!"
The Lawyer: "Question, pause, answer, stop!"

Understanding the Conversation Gap

Regardless of the audience for our communication, we are used to—and pride ourselves in—a form of communication that is informal and fun: conversation. Casual, interesting, and free-flowing, good conversation is an integral part of our day, our relationships, and even our self-esteem.

There is a wonderful quotation from a 19th-century French writer, describing conversation as: "[t]he art of never seeming wearisome, of knowing how to invest every trifle with interest, to charm no matter what be the subject, and to fascinate with absolutely nothing."[1] All of us would love to be so graceful.

Yet, consider the gap between this and being a witness. Conversation is casual because the setting is informal, but what if it was all under oath? Conversation is interesting because we can be open and creative, but what if every word was being transcribed? Conversation is free-flowing because

---

1. GUY DE MAUPASSANT, SUR L'EAU (ON THE FACE OF THE WATERS (President Publishing Co., 1881).

we feel free to say whatever we want, but what if every word, once tran-scribed, would be picked apart, and used against us or others in the future? Those three things—the oath, the transcription, and the follow-up—are the reasons this gap is so difficult. This is *not* a conversation!

All the wonderful qualities de Maupassant finds in a conversation are not appropriate for a witness. If conversation is an art, then being a wit-ness is a science. If the goal in conversation is to be interesting, the goal of a witness is to be precise. A witness is not there to entertain, just to tell "nothing but the truth" in a clear, simple way. If doing this feels boring or uncomfortable, that's far better than being charming but in trouble because you said too much.

A good conversation, we say, flows along well, and a good conversa-tionalist is someone who listens to where it's going, and helps it get there. Good testimony, alas, does not flow. It is very awkward and stop-and-start: question, pause, answer, stop—then start all over again. A good listener as a witness is not someone who focuses on what the questioner meant, or where he or she is going, but only on the words that came out of the ques-tioner's mouth—the words the court reporter heard.

Some time ago, I represented an international sales manager, a brilliant man who spoke several languages fluently. However, by the time he finished preparing for and giving testimony, he volunteered to me that this was the hardest new language he had learned—not because of the words themselves, but because of the unnatural and artificial discipline required.

This is not a conversation!

Bridging the Conversation Gap

Several years ago, the TV series *The West Wing* had a series of episodes about a scandal in the White House. The president had multiple sclero-sis, and he and his advisers did not disclose it. The news has now broken, and an investigation has been launched into whether top aides broke the law in covering up this fact. The president's press secretary, C.J., has been subpoenaed to testify and has been called to meet with the White House counsel to prepare.

C.J. is intelligent and talkative. She is clearly nervous and angry about the situation—both being called as a witness and having to meet with counsel. Unable to do much about her frustration, she takes it out on counsel by being sarcastic, uncooperative, and not eager to take advice. Counsel is trying to make her understand the need to prepare. Then, in the middle of talking about what happened, he stops, and there is roughly this exchange:

Counsel: Do you know what time it is?
C.J.: It's five past noon.
Counsel: I'd like you to get out of the habit of doing that!
C.J.: Doing what?
Counsel: Answering more than was asked!
(Pause.)
Do you know what time it is?
(Long pause.)
C.J.: Yes.
Counsel: Now we're making progress. We'll take a break and meet again later today.

If you teach your witness nothing else, teach him or her the answer to the question "Do you know what time it is?" because the answer is the difference between a conversation and testimony. In a conversation, questions are not really questions—they're prompts, a means of moving the conversation in a particular direction. It's rare that people are really looking for the precise answer or will be offended if they don't get it. As a result, in a conversation, the answer yes, the accurate answer, the precise answer, is a bad one. That's not what the questioner meant. That's not where the conversation is flowing. In a testimony environment, the question *is* important, and yes is the right answer. "Do you know what time it is?" That *is* what the questioner *asked*. Answer: yes. That is the core difference between a normal conversation and a testimony environment.

Chapter 7

The Control Gap

Defining the Control Gap

The Witness: "It's their deposition; I just have to sit here and take it."
The Lawyer: "Why is he letting this questioner walk all over him?"

Understanding the Control Gap

Even to highly accomplished individuals who are well accustomed to being in command of every situation, the witness chair gives all the appearances of the questioner being in control: it is his subpoena, his case, his arena, his life's work. The questioner walks in with a list—written or in his head—of questions designed to trip up the witness, along with a variety of battle-tested follow-up techniques if the prepared questions don't work. It seems obvious who's in control.

However, if the witness—or the witness's counsel—buys into this deception, they put themselves at a terrible disadvantage. What lawyer and client need to understand is that all that impressive stuff is just that: it's just stuff, designed to get the witness's testimony. This is all about the witness's testimony, and so witnesses have the right and the responsibility to control their own testimony. Witnesses cannot tell the truth as they know it—not as the questioner would mold it—unless they are in control.

Bridging the Control Gap

Control here does not mean emotion or volume. Most witnesses have plenty of experience with other forms of interaction with strangers—meetings, conference calls, and so on. These interactions are rarely controlled by who shouts the loudest. They are controlled by a set of rules—stated or just understood—of professionalism and courtesy. The same applies here. The witness is there to answer questions, but the questions—and the answers—must be clear, simple, and fair. It is up to the witness to impose this discipline. Counsel needs to help the witness understand this deceptive environment and provide the witness with a framework of rules to take control of his or her own testimony.

Chapter 8

Preparing Ourselves

Goals

Before we prepare a witness, we as lawyers must prepare ourselves. If we are to become effective advocates for our clients, we must first take the necessary steps to ensure that we are adequately prepared to prepare the client, develop the case, and present the case before the judge or jury if appropriate. The primary goals of lawyer preparation can be referred to as the Three Cs: control, credibility, and confidence.

Control means being prepared and organized enough to minimize groping and fumbling. Murphy's Law always applies in a deposition room, courtroom, or other legal setting. Anything that can go wrong will go wrong. The more prepared we are and the more prepared our witnesses are, the fewer the problems that will arise, and the better we will be able to deal with the inevitable disasters that come up in litigation.

Credibility means being prepared to the extent that the witness is more inclined to trust you, the judge is more inclined to rule for you, the other side is less inclined to challenge you, and the jury or finder of fact is more inclined to believe in you. That means being prepared and organized enough to know that if you say something, it's correct and clearly supported.

Confidence does not mean not being nervous. Confidence means being prepared and organized in such a way that you walk into court knowing that you are prepared to encounter any potential obstacle.

Some years ago there was a series of commercials for a line of pasta sauce. The tag line at the end of each of the ads was always "It's in there," meaning that whatever you might need or want in a pasta sauce is in that jar. With good preparation, you should think about your trial notebook or witness notebook in that way. You should have the comfort, control, and confidence to think, "It's in there." The end result of this preparation is *command* of the courtroom or other witness environment.

Methods

In order to achieve confidence, control, and credibility, we must first step back a little. We want to think about the witness before getting too intensely involved in a case, because once we are involved, it is easy to lose sight of the forest for the trees. To begin preparing a witness we have to think broadly about that witness. Broaden your perspective about who the witness is, what he or she really knows, and what he or she has to offer to help prepare to teach the fact finder. To reach this command of the facts and the witness, remember the acronym BOSS, which stands for *brainstorming, organizing, storytelling,* and *simplifying.*

Brainstorming means just that. Think about each witness or client from the broadest possible perspective. What does that client have to say? What has that client done? What are that client's issues? What is good about the client? What is bad about the client? What kind of image is that client going to portray as a witness and is that the kind of image you? Where does the client fit in the broader picture? What does he know about the case? What doesn't he know? What does he think he knows and what would you like him to think he knows? Those are distinctly different things in any case.

Organizing means to determine what items you need in order to prepare that witness. In order to work with each witness, you need core documents, including a witness list containing key information, such as contact information. You also need a working file for each witness and an exhibit list detailing who will introduce or use each exhibit and listing the exhibits that correspond to the witness file.

Additionally, you should have a chronology for every case within your file and a case outline that summarizes and includes relevant elements and defenses of the case, a list of evidence that will be used, and a review of the key issues. These are not just pieces of paper. They are your assistants. Regardless of how many people you have on your team, these core documents are essential assistants in the process.

Storytelling is something we often forget to do. By storytelling, I mean talking to other people about your witness and about your witness's predicament, in order to get a broader understanding of the issues that may become problematic at trial. It is fine to talk to other lawyers. But if that is all you are doing, you are not preparing adequately. Real storytelling means talking to nonlawyers. This is important because you are preparing witnesses—generally—to talk to nonlawyers. Even if you are preparing them for a deposition, you are not really preparing them to speak to the other side's lawyer; you are preparing them to tell a story that will eventually be going to the finder of fact.

I once tried a case in which the effect of what's called winter ice accumulating on a commercial fishing boat out in cold weather was a key issue. It took some storytelling for us to realize that this important concept in the case did not mean anything to most people. We said winter ice and most people thought of a glaze on the road or pretty icicles that form on the eaves on a cold day. In fact, the commercial fishing boats involved would go out to sea for several months at a time and would gather up to *ten tons* of ice on every exposed part of the rigging and the top part of the boat. The winter ice was so severe that often a crewmember was assigned to go out and hack away at the ice with an ax. It took talking about the case with a number of people to realize that people didn't understand this. Storytelling showed us that we had to find ways of drawing a better picture of winter ice.

Simplifying means to focus on what is most important. After we have done all of the brainstorming, organizing, and storytelling, we need to eliminate the excess details. You want to introduce the witness and her story, but there is danger in having too much detail. With too much detail you run the risk of losing sight of what is really important and losing the jury's attention. After you create your outline, you must simplify by focusing on the key issues and determining what you need to discuss with your witness.

Tools

Witness Notebook

The basic tool for preparing yourself is the witness notebook, a 3-ring binder that can hold paper, dividers, and plastic sleeves. I am, I confess, a notebook fanatic. There are other ways to get organized, but few are better than a notebook. For every witness, no matter how large or how small, you should have a separate witness notebook. Index cards are for indexes, and notepads are for taking notes. Neither is an organizational tool. A notebook is an organizational tool. It holds your witness outline firmly. Any document that is important enough to reference is important enough to put into your witness notebook, along with extra courtroom copies in a plastic sleeve. Every subject has numbered dividers and those numbers correspond to a table of contents in the front. So, if you are talking to a witness about a particular subject, or if you are in court or in a deposition and a particular subject is addressed, you can take out the notebook and go right to the section for that subject matter. Additionally, if you are going to take notes during testimony, get a standard-size three-hole punched pad, so that your notes can go directly into the witness notebook.

Witness Outline

Whether you are questioning a witness or preparing one, the key document is a witness outline. A sample page of my suggested format for a witness outline is included in appendix A. The witness outline contains one subject matter per page. The subject heading is numbered and corresponds to the Table of Contents. The text should always be in large type, with generous spacing. You should draw a line two-thirds of the way over on the right-hand side and a line toward the bottom. On the left-hand side of the page are the notes for questions or anticipated questions. The questions should be indicated in short bullets. There should be no full sentences, no question marks, and nothing that is more than three words long. These are simply topics. You are creating a checklist of the things to ask that witness. Why such simplicity? Because there is a magnetic attraction between your eye and the written word. The more you write down on the page, whether it is sitting in a room with a witness or questioning the witness on the witness stand, the more you are going to be reading what is on the page and the less you are going to be paying attention to that witness. The only exceptions to this general rule are questions that are either foundational ("Is this being kept in the ordinary course of business?") or hypotheticals presented to an expert witness.

The right-hand side of the witness notebook is for your notations. Anything that backs up the questions you are asking goes on the right side of the line. Every reference and any exhibit or citation that relates to a question you intend to ask should be noted on the right side of the witness outline. For example, references to depositions or other transcripts, with page and live numbers, should be noted on the right side, if they relate to the questions that are being asked. You should anticipate legal issues regarding evidence, procedure, theory, and relevance, and prepare accordingly. The other item that goes on the right side of the line are the notes to yourself. You should include items that will help you during the trial or deposition. If you tend to talk too fast, write "slow down." If you wander around too much, write "stand still." These are your notes. They are for your eyes only.

If a document is worth mentioning in your witness outline, it is also worth including in the notebook. You should "mark up" one copy of the document and place it in the notebook. Then, take three copies for the witness, the court, and opposing counsel (or more depending on how many lawyers are going to be involved in the event you are attending) and put them in a plastic sleeve, to ensure that everything you need is right there.

The bottom section of the witness outline should include your citations. If there is an issue of law you think may come up, you should address it in the witness outline and have relevant case and/or law citations included at the bottom of the page. If it is a key point, you could prepare what we call a mini-memo, which is literally a one-page memo about the relevant law that expands on it slightly. Put it in your notebook, with copies in a plastic sleeve. If you are prepared to counter an objection with a mini-memo for the court, you will probably not get as many objections, and if you do get objections, the judge is more likely to trust you because she will believe, since you are prepared, that what you need and what she needs to rule on the issue is "in there." Being prepared in this way allows you to present the issue to the judge in a way that increases your credibility.

This system can be used whether you are dealing with a small case with only one witness or a large, complex case with dozens of witnesses. Every notebook is an independent, complete, and separate item. While the size and number of notebooks will change, the concept stays the same.

While this system has been used by lawyers for many years, it is not any one system in particular that is essential. What is more important is that you develop your own system that you feel comfortable with, and then use it religiously. Consistency is the key, so that every time you open up the notebook, what you see on the page is comforting and familiar to you. Every time you open the witness notebook, no matter what the situation, no matter how frazzled you are, you can have confidence that if you have adequately prepared, what you are looking for is "in there."

Chapter 9

Understanding the Audience

Regardless of who is in the room for the witness's testimony—lawyers at a deposition, investigators at an interview, and so on—the ultimate audience for that testimony is generally the finder of fact. That finder of fact comes in various forms, but it is most often a jury, so it is important to examine and understand that audience.

It has become fashionable to bash juries. Certainly, there are examples of juries doing irrational or foolish things. Strangely enough, they have good company in that: lawyers, doctors, business tycoons, and even politicians have all been guilty of similar flaws. Perhaps when we refer to a jury of our peers, we should accept that that means imperfect human beings, capable of the best and worst in all of us.

In fact, though, I have found that juries are capable of great collective wisdom. Most jurors genuinely want to do a good job and to do the right thing. I don't like to talk about jurors as an amorphous blob. Help your witness understand by personalizing Juror #6. Describe him or her in a way that means something to your witness, and then pose the challenge "How do we reach Juror #6?" A large part of the job of both counsel and witness is to teach jurors your case. They are willing students. If a willing student doesn't learn adequately, whose fault is that: student or teacher?

How to Help the Audience Understand Your Case

Humanize the Witness

Too often, questions about a witness's background become a dull formality, quickly run through and barely heard by the jury. This is a wasted opportunity. Every witness has stories—little or large—that help better explain their character and life choices. It is important to work with your witness in preparation, probe for those stories, and then make sure they come out in testimony to put flesh on the bare bones of background.

As just one of many examples, I have had the privilege of working with a number of nursing home administrators. They are, generally, very special people, doing extraordinary work. They deal constantly with sometimes frazzled staff, difficult vendors, needy patients, and troubled family. Yet, like all of us, they get up every day, get dressed, eat breakfast, and go to work. It is their routine, and an unprepared witness can make it sound routine when it is not.

That sense of complacency is made dramatically worse by language and misconceptions. The title "administrator" carries a certain image for Juror #6. The image is like the title character in the cartoon *Dilbert*: a nameless, faceless bureaucrat who sits in a cubicle, and moves paper from the inbox to the outbox. Nothing could be further from the truth, but it means that the witness has the burden of finding opportunities to move Juror #6 from misconceptions to reality.

Consider answers to the same question from two different depositions of nursing home administrators. The first:

Q. What kind of contact do you have with the residents at your facility?
A. I have regular contact with them.

This is an appropriate, clear, and truthful answer. Short and sweet. But that is exactly the problem. While it answers the question in a general way, it does nothing to help Juror #6 overcome his or her misconceptions. A petty bureaucrat might have regular contact of a meaningless sort. It is a significant lost opportunity to help bring out the truth and humanize the witness.

Now, consider the same question, but in a different deposition, where the witness understood the need to use those opportunities to bring humanity to a dehumanizing deposition process.

Q. What kind of contact do you have with the residents at your facility?
A. I don't know. How many days do you have? I have a lot contact with the residents. I fall in love every day. I cry a lot when we lose a resident. I'm privileged to be a part of their lives. I'm privileged to work with their families. I'm privileged to be a part of a team that provides service for a family and a resident so that the time that they spend with their loved one is quality time. It's not time consumed with worrying about changing, bathing, and doing other things that the family members would have to do. And I'm privileged to be a part of a team that does that and loves to do it. And we all treasure our interactions with the residents, be it an activity, be it our little—one lady who sits in the hallway, and you go by, and you say hi to her. She's the angel in the hallway. She's a little hall monitor doing her little find-a-words. Or be it a confused patient who just wants you to sit down and talk to her and listen.
Q. And going back to the—changing topics for a second—back to computer e-mail. I missed something.
A. Was I boring you?

Slowly, Juror #6 gets to know and appreciate the witness as a person. Meanwhile, opposing counsel clearly understands the impact. This is a case about patient care, the administrator is talking about that care, but opposing counsel wants to get her off that topic and "back to computer e-mail." Humanize the witness.

Humanize the Party

If the parties to the controversy go beyond your witness, then it becomes important to tell their story as well. Find the stories that turn entities from faceless bureaucracies to good citizens, interesting success stories, and whatever else can help Juror #6 see beyond corporate symbols, documents, and financials.

Simplify the Language

Neither lawyer nor witness can expect to teach Juror #6, if you speak a language he or she does not understand. Lawyers sometimes see jargon as a problem for expert witnesses. But we *all* have jargon; it may come from our profession, our occupation, our upbringing, our region, and more. Jargon stops the learning process dead in its tracks; not only does the listener not understand what is being said, but he or she may spend the next few minutes trying to figure it out, thereby missing what comes next. Or the listener may just turn off entirely. Regardless, Juror #6 becomes that much less interested in what the witness has to say.

Simplify the Message

Counsel may have spent weeks, months, even years delving into every aspect and detail of the case. The witness may have lived with the subject matter for far longer. Both know so much about it that it often becomes too much. Buried in detail, they miss the forest for all the trees. Preparing a witness means simplifying the message—bringing it back down to the fundamentals of what is truly at issue.

As a young prosecutor, many years ago, I went through a training program that put me in traffic court. I learned all the various rules and regulations relating to the stop sign. But out on the road, it's the sign itself that matters, not the details. Many years later, working with witnesses in a large products liability "failure to warn" case, I read transcripts with endless debate about what should or should not be on warning labels. Finally, I brought in a stop sign and said, "This is a warning label; the rest is just information." If the warning label in this case says not to do it, we should be comfortable with that—the rest is just detail.

Chapter 10

Three Mistakes Witnesses Make

When someone is called to be a witness of any kind, no book or other outsider's advice can replace the need for effective preparation. This seems obvious to anyone who has experience dealing with this question-and-answer format. However, it is not so obvious to many lawyers or laypeople. There are lots of seemingly good excuses for a potential witness not to bother with preparation. Let's consider three of the most common, and how counsel can respond.

1. "I'll Just Tell My Story."

A party to litigation is convinced he or she knows the case and doesn't need outside interference. For someone who is not a party or a target but just an outside observer, being a witness can be a large and disruptive imposition. The notion of spending even more time just preparing to be a witness can seem like an unnecessary burden. Moreover, since the witness knows what the truth is, why does he or she need someone else's advice on what to say? In light of all this, the temptation to just go in and tell your story without preparation can be great. It can also be an invitation to disaster.

Consider the Questioner's Advantages

Both lawyer and client must understand that the main goal of preparation is to level the playing field on which the client will be questioned. Otherwise, it is an extraordinarily unbalanced field. Think about all the advantages that most questioners have before they walk in:

Experience

Whether the questioner is a lawyer, investigator, or other professional, he or she has probably spent a lifetime of education, training, and experience preparing to question witnesses. This is what these questioners do for a living. What is unnatural to the witness is natural to them, and they have spent a career learning to ask questions in what will seem like a strange new language.

Preparation

The questioner may have spent days, weeks, months, or even years working on this matter. The questioner has explored, inside and out, a subject area that is only a vague memory to everyone else.

Documents

The questioner has reviewed the relevant documents carefully and is ready to compare any answers to those documents.

Other Witnesses

The questioner probably has questioned or plans to question others in the matter, using previous responses to generate new questions to ask and comparing all answers under a microscope.

Script

Most important, pulling together all of these advantages, the questioner has then spent time specifically preparing the questions. The questioner may have a script or a list of questions, documents ready to show, and other ways to make sure to be prepared. The questioner knows where the proceeding is going; the witness does not.

Don't Walk in Unprepared

A potential witness *and* his or her lawyer should think carefully about the questioner's advantages. How much preparation has the *witness* done? Let's assume that you don't act foolishly in other important matters. Why would anyone be foolish enough to ignore all these advantages and just walk in unprepared? The reality is that there are no shortcuts here. Spending time on preparation is the only way to make the time your client spends being questioned less painful, more effective, and ultimately shorter.

Many witnesses have "the curse of the intelligent witness." Remember, the proceeding is *not* a conversation. Most of the things that make intelligent people—including many professionals like lawyers and doctors—such good conversationalists often make them terrible witnesses. It is simply a very different skill set. They talk too much and too fast; they volunteer information; they draw inferences and conclusions; they preach, argue, and explain. Mostly, they think out loud; they speak without thinking first. It is a dangerous, downhill spiral.

You are walking into a strange and unnatural environment, with a great deal at stake, where everyone else is experienced, comfortable, and prepared. You cannot adequately prepare for this challenge without professional help. Period. Some of the best salesmen, orators, thinkers, and executives have the toughest time making the transition to this unnatural environment. Lawyers, of course, are among them.

2. "It's Too Expensive."

Expense takes many forms: time, money, anxiety, and more. Being a witness can take an enormous amount of each—too much, in many people's eyes.

Bill Gates, Kenneth Lay, Martha Stewart, Scooter Libby, Bill Clinton, Dennis Koslowski—the list goes on and on: a parade of extraordinarily intelligent and successful people who have had disastrous experiences as witnesses. Why? Witness preparation is not a distraction: it's an investment—in the past, present, and future. It's an investment in the past, to try to address and ultimately bring closure to prior issues. It's an investment in the present, to make this witness experience as manageable and successful as possible. It's an investment in the future, to avoid mistakes or bad testimony that can lead to future depositions and/or other expensive, time-consuming litigation steps. Unprepared testimony is a bad—and dangerous—investment.

Time. Even if someone else is paying a witness's legal fees (for example, an employer, liability insurer, or directors and officers liability insurer), that cannot make up for the hours and days lost in both preparation and actual testimony. However, inadequate preparation can lead to poor testimony, and that can be not only far more painful and time-consuming to give, it can return to haunt the witness in so many ways. Bad testimony is the gift that keeps on giving. Take the time now in order to avoid having to take the time later.

Money. No doubt about it, legal fees today are extraordinarily high. If the witness has to pay a lawyer, it adds a new dimension of pain to an already burdensome experience. However, the real issue with cost is always relative. Is true preparation expensive? Yes. Is it *too* expensive? That's a relative term. As we say when we prepare witnesses, the response should always be, "Compared to what?" What's the alternative? Saving time and money up-front by being a witness without counsel or without extensive preparation can cost dearly later in time, money, and heartache. This is too important. This is the wrong time and place to try to save.

3. "I Didn't Do Anything Wrong."

This is the toughest and the most common misperception. Most people think that you need a lawyer only if you've done something wrong, particularly in the witness environment. Even people who use lawyers all the time for real estate, business, or other purposes may have this common notion that as witnesses, they need a lawyer only if they have done something wrong. Counsel has to understand this misperception, then help the witness to get around it.

Certainly, there are times when a lawyer serves as a "defender" of a client who has done something "wrong." However, the reach of investigations, litigation, and other inquiries today is incredibly broad, and definitions of what is "wrong" vary just as widely. A client needs help in navigating this mess. I tell clients to think of me as their tour guide through this strange and dangerous jungle. Given the harm that can come to people as a result of these inquiries, whether or not they've done anything wrong, a witness is foolish to enter this world alone. As the old maps of the world used to say in describing unknown waters, "This way be dragons."

Moreover, even if the witness "hasn't done anything wrong" *before* getting onto the witness stand, the testimony *itself* may create a wide range of issues or problems. For example, the witness usually won't know what has gone on in the matter before, or who has said what to whom. A lawyer may be able to find out, through joint defense agreements and other avenues, and help the witness avoid unnecessary conflicts and other pitfalls. In this and other ways, a lawyer can help guide the client through this risky process as safely as possible.

A potential witness should never feel awkward or defensive about undertaking extensive preparation. It's the witness's right, and it's the right thing to do.

Finally, having chosen a lawyer to prepare with, it is critical that the client use that person exclusively. The client should not talk to anyone else about the matter. No other conversation is privileged, and questioners often love to ask, "Who else did you talk to about this matter?" For clients who are uncomfortable explaining this to some people, I suggest making the lawyer the bad guy: "Gosh, I'd love to talk about this with you, but my lawyer told me I can't." Otherwise, they open themselves (and those they speak with) to unnecessary questioning.

If you listen carefully to a witness's reluctance to properly prepare you will usually hear some version of these three mistakes. Help your witness to understand and overcome them, and you will help the witness level the playing field and succeed in this difficult and unnatural environment.

Chapter 11

Seven Mistakes Lawyers Make

Before a lawyer can convince a client to take on the burden of preparation, the lawyer has to be convinced it is necessary. Unfortunately, while law schools and continuing legal education programs may do a good job of teaching legal principles and theory, they often ignore the true focus of real-world legal practice: the client. Just like the political campaign whose mantra "It's the Economy, Stupid!" served as a reminder of what was most important, law schools should perhaps add "It's the Client, Stupid!" to the inspirational Latin phrases that adorn their ivy halls.

For now, the reality is that too few places really teach lawyers how to deal with clients, and they certainly do not teach lawyers how to help clients navigate something as difficult and foreign as the process of being a witness. The commonly accepted notion that lawyers will somehow pick up these types of skills as they go along is dangerous nonsense. At best, it is a recipe for a long trial-and-error learning process, and real clients with serious problems are the guinea pigs. As a profession, we can do better in this important area.

Meanwhile, even experienced lawyers may share some common misperceptions that can account for their failure to prepare a client or witness adequately. A failure in preparation is a failure in representation. Don't make these same mistakes.

1. "I'm Too Busy."

No matter how busy you are, it's hard to ignore a formally scheduled deposition or other appearance as a witness. Yet, it's often too easy for a lawyer to ignore the preparation stage. After all, the client usually doesn't understand the importance of preparation, and the lawyer has other more immediate demands on his or her time. However, you are not properly representing your client if you allow the client to make an appearance as a witness without *thorough* preparation. You must find the time to work together, or don't take on the representation.

There are some ways that you can make the time you spend more efficient. For example, give the client the appropriate introduction memo to read in advance. Encourage your client to read it carefully before your next meeting and to write any comments or questions on it. Then use it as a basis for discussion every time you meet. Second, have an associate or paralegal organize documents, create an outline of the matter to serve as a base, and even conduct the practice questions. Still, nothing can replace the substantial time commitment required for this process.

Some years ago, as general counsel to a national health-care company, I gave a talk on litigation to a group of doctors, with particular emphasis on the importance of careful preparation before giving any testimony or statements. Toward the end of my talk, a doctor in the back raised his hand and said, "That sounds great, but when I had to give a deposition recently, my lawyer called me up and told me to meet him a half hour before my testimony, and we'd prepare then. What should I have done?"

What lawyers should understand—even though clients have no reason to—is that that's not preparation, that's malpractice. Get another lawyer. Preparing someone for the unnatural and challenging witness environment takes a commitment of time and effort from both lawyer and client.

2. "The Client Is Too Busy."

Many clients don't see, or don't want to see, how vital good witness preparation is for them. They don't want to take the time out of their busy lives to pay a lawyer to help them do something that they don't think they need help doing in the first place. The lawyer must accept the obligation to push—sometimes hard—to overcome this reluctance. None of us like to push a client this way, but we are not doing our jobs if we don't push. The most important battle we fight *for* our clients is sometimes *with* our clients.

Again, there are ways to work with the client to help accommodate the competing demands of preparation time and a busy schedule. Nights and weekends may sometimes be the best available times. Although preparation is best done in blocks of uninterrupted time that may last several hours, I have in some instances conducted pieces of the process during long flights, on limousine rides, and even via international telephone calls. Flexibility goes only so far though. The quest for time can be a constant one, but it is necessary.

3. "All Witnesses Are Created Equal."

Part of the challenge of properly preparing witnesses is that it cannot be done in a standardized, cookie-cutter way. A client recently told me of a prior experience in which she had to give a deposition in a discrimination case brought by someone else against her employer. Her employer's lawyer "represented" her (with no apparent regard to the conflict issues) and in preparation merely gave her what was clearly a canned speech, having little to do with the sensitive issues in that case. In fact, witnesses differ enormously depending on their background, personality, education, experience as a witness, profession, and involvement in the issues or events being addressed. What might be appropriate preparation for one witness may be useless gibberish to another. You must adapt your preparation accordingly.

To properly prepare a witness, counsel must do their homework. *Learn* about the client's business or other matters relating to the inquiry. Part of the challenge of any litigation is learning about a new world—a new product, profession, technology, or whatever. To prepare a witness, you not only have to learn the new world, you have to *understand* it. You have to go beyond just learning the jargon to understanding the way business is done: how things really work, what the real issues and procedures are, what roles different people play. For example, a client's position on an organizational chart may not accurately reflect his or her real authority or responsibilities. You need to ask questions of your client and do your own research to truly understand this new world.

Understand the client's personality, background, and needs. Clients facing the prospect of being a witness may come to you displaying a full range of emotions and attitudes, from overwrought to overconfident. The irony is that once you get to know them better, you may find that the initially overwrought client may make a good witness, while the overconfident client may make a lousy witness. Clients bring with them an enormous range of insecurities and fears about being questioned, knowledge of and familiarity with legal proceedings, and willingness and ability to learn.

4. "You Never Know What They'll Ask."

Lawyers sometimes limit their preparation—either intentionally or unwittingly—because they don't know how to anticipate what a questioner will ask. They reassure their clients by assuring them that such ignorance is normal: "You never know. . . ." However, the fact that you rarely know *all* of the questions doesn't mean you cannot anticipate and prepare for *many* of them. We cannot eliminate every surprise that our clients may face, but we can and should help minimize the number and severity of those surprises. There are a variety of ways that a lawyer can, in fact, know what they'll ask. They include the following.

Wear the Opponent's Hat
Constantly challenge yourself, those working with you, and even your clients to put on the other side's hat. How would we view a set of facts from their side? What questions would we want to ask? Brainstorm these issues with and without the client present. If resources allow it, assign someone to play that role and prepare questions accordingly.

Use What's Out There
Whatever the nature of the process, there are likely to be prior transcripts, discovery, or standard guides or manuals (sometimes CLE materials) that

will help you to understand and anticipate at least the general outlines of the questioner's approach. Have you fully researched the other side or the issues on the Internet?

Use Their Stuff

One of the side effects of big government is that bureaucracies often develop strategies secretly in one office and disclose them publicly in another. Some agencies' in-house manuals are actually published, such as *The U.S. Department of Justice Manual* (published by Prentice-Hall), which includes the standard Advice of Rights for grand jury witnesses and other grand jury information. Other agencies require you to work a little harder. For example, the internal manual of the Securities and Exchange Commission (SEC), *Guide to Taking Testimony in Investigative Proceedings*, has been available through the Freedom of Information Act. It contains the SEC's standard script of questions, which helps to prepare witnesses for the kind of extraordinary detail that the SEC pursues in almost every case.

Use Other Lawyers

Who else has been questioned or has testified in the matter? As a lawyer, you can make contacts lawyer-to-lawyer that might be awkward for the client. You may be able to get file memos, transcripts, or just oral reports from counsel of what was asked of others and what might be asked of your client.

5. Preaching, Rather Than Teaching

You can tell a client the required language for a legal document, or what forms must be filed with a particular agency or court, but you cannot *tell* a client how to be a witness. That has to be taught. Doing this successfully means avoiding lecturing and preaching, and instead, using a variety of methods to work together toward understanding. "Just do as I say" rarely works with our children on even simple things; it certainly won't work with clients on this far more difficult subject.

The key here is one of the same things that we tell clients: *Listen.* Invite questions, ask for feedback, ask questions, and generally do whatever it takes to make sure that you understand what *this* client needs in *this* situation. If you get on a roll, talking at your client, *stop* to ask for questions, or to see what else would help. The client might be helped by being given more examples, more time to review the summary memo and then discuss it, or more practice questions. Real learning happens in that kind of back-and-forth exchange.

6. "The Law Is the Law."

As a lawyer, you have spent three years of law school and the span of your career—however long it has been—learning to speak a strange language: legalese. To help a client understand the challenges and choices he or she faces as a witness, you must relearn English. The more legal issues that are involved in the matter, or in your client's appearance, the harder you have to try to avoid legalese. A client who has learned the legal terms—but not what they mean—truly has learned just enough to be dangerous.

Advise the client every step of the way based on a full understanding and careful analysis of the law and the facts. The process of being a witness, as well as the questions a client may be asked as a witness, may expose the client to a wide variety of risks: criminal, civil, financial, employment- or family-related, and more. As counsel, you need to be constantly on guard against these risks and ready to discuss them openly with your client when they arise. Being called as a witness can often lead to a difficult balancing of risks and opportunities, which requires your client's best wisdom and judgment—at a moment's notice. It's up to you to prepare your client to be able to avoid those risks and to take advantage of the opportunities.

Guide the client through a sometimes strange and terrifying legal maze. From childhood, we are scared of the dark because we do not know what's out there. For most people, being a witness is like being in darkness: they don't know how to get through it, but they do know that there are monsters and other dangers lurking out there. You have to be aware of this, and take care to explain and guide the client through each step, knowing that what may seem to you the smallest, most routine step may look like an unfathomable leap to your client.

7. "Do I Need to Draw You a Road Map?"

Yes, you do! I am constantly amazed (and pleased, when I am the questioner) to encounter witnesses who may have been prepared on the facts, and perhaps even on how to answer questions, but who have not been prepared on the simple mechanics of what's going to happen. As a result, they walk into a strange room in front of strange people and are intimidated and overwhelmed by the most basic logistics or procedures. They quickly become shaken up, whatever preparation they did is largely lost, and they start the questioning at a severe disadvantage from which they may never recover.

There is nothing condescending to witnesses about being careful to prepare them thoroughly. Take the time to walk through exactly what the witness can expect and do it slowly, step by step, allowing lots of time for questions. Start with the basics: who, what, when, where, and why. Then go through each phase of what will happen and apply these same questions: Is it recorded or transcribed? Is it videotaped? Is it under oath? Who will be there? Who will ask questions? Who should I look at? Who should I talk to? And so on. Being a witness is a strange and frightening experience regardless of the preparation. Part of counsel's job is to make it less strange (and hopefully less frightening) by making it more familiar.

On some level, all lawyers know that preparation is important. But there are so many easy excuses to get in the way, and clients are rarely sophisticated enough to understand what's happening—and what's wrong. Don't fall prey to those temptations. Find the time and make the effort to do it right.

Chapter 12

What Preparation Means

Mistakes of Preparation

Too many lawyers—including some very good ones—do not prepare witnesses adequately because they fail to understand how dramatically different being a witness is from anything else the client has experienced. Testimony is not a conversation. Much of what makes for a good conversation makes for bad testimony. And what it takes to be a good witness is often contrary to our typical experiences.

As a result, serving as a witness requires an extraordinary level of preparation. Too many lawyers' idea of preparation falls short in at least two key ways:

- It is not comprehensive enough.
- It is not tough enough.

Not Comprehensive Enough

It happens too often: we've been working hard to prepare a witness for hours, or days, and the witness expresses surprise at the length and integrity of the process. Their prior exposure to witness preparation may have been a hurried conference, a confusing memo, a short meeting with a junior lawyer or paralegal, or some other shortcut. However, true witness preparation is an extensive—and intensive—multistep process. It demands a high level of time, energy, and effort from *both* client and counsel.

Not Tough Enough

Lawyers do not serve their witnesses well by being too kind and gentle in preparation. On the contrary, I tell witnesses that the tougher and more realistic we are with them, the better prepared they will be for the real thing. At the end of the whole process, every witness should come out of the real experience and say what many of our witnesses say to us: "You guys were much tougher!" That's a sign of success and it's high praise. Make it happen.

Seven Steps for Preparing the Witness

There are seven key steps to the preparation process, each requiring careful thought and thorough implementation.

1. Start with an Introduction

Imagine sitting down on a park bench and having a total stranger come up and ask you about your most private details and troubling secrets. You'd think they were crazy, and certainly wouldn't answer in any depth. Why are we as lawyers so arrogant that we think we can do that with someone just because they have the label of "client" or "witness"? You can't; it won't work. You're a stranger, no matter what the environment, whether you're representing them personally or you're an agency or corporate lawyer. The fact that you're a stranger makes them doubly uncomfortable.

Take the time to get to know your witness and get comfortable with each other, both before you meet, through other people or the Internet, and at the outset of the meeting. What do you need to know about your client's background, interests, and family? What does the client need to know about yours? How can you find a common bond? The time invested up-front to do this is well worth it.

Earn the trust and faith of the client. This is a circular process: the more confidence your client has in you, the more he or she will listen to you and the more help you can be when the client is on the witness stand. However, that trust and faith does not automatically spring from the fact that you are a lawyer or that you have a nice office with diplomas on the wall. You have to earn that kind of relationship, just as you would have to earn it in the outside world—except that with your client, you have far less time to develop that relationship. Foremost throughout this process is the need to communicate clearly and effectively. There is so much that needs to be communicated about both the substance and the process that good communication becomes not just a means to an end, but an end in itself.

Witnesses will often be asked questions about things that are private, difficult, embarrassing, or worse. We cannot truly expect—or demand—meaningful communication on such sensitive areas, from a complete stranger. Counsel must consider what *they* would need from a stranger in such an environment, to even begin to open up. Without taking the time and effort to establish that bond, everything else may just be going through the motions.

2. Review the Facts

Encourage your witnesses to go over as much as they know about the likely subject matter of the questioning: who, what, when, where, why, and how? What do they remember, and what might someone else remember? Going through it one time is rarely enough. Go back over the facts in slow motion to catch more of the details and issues. I tell witnesses that if you watch sports on TV, the action is repeated in slow motion because in real time it happens too fast for most people to follow and understand. The players on the field may follow it and understand it, but for someone who isn't part of it, it happens too fast. Nor can anyone talk about it and explain it as fast as it happens. The same concept applies here.

Reviewing the facts usually includes reviewing the documents and exhibits. I know there are some arguments to the contrary, but on balance it is very important to show the witness the important documents and take the time to discuss issues of credibility, language, and context (and "spin"). However, be clear with the witness that this is not school; the witness will not be graded on how much he or she memorized. This is just to get the witness comfortable with some of the documents and allow you to ask questions about them. It is *not* a substitute for being careful about documents in the deposition, and reading them!

If the witness is asked questions about what documents have been reviewed, it may not be appropriate for the witness to answer. This varies somewhat by jurisdiction, but I believe that a lawyer's decisions regarding which documents among many are important enough to show the witness in preparation is itself a work product–privileged decision, and in that case, the witness should not answer. If the local rules and/or practices allow such questions, prepare your witness for them. Also, remind the witness of Rule 6: If you don't remember, say so. You've shown the witness a lot of document but this is not some silly memory contest. If the most truthful answer is, "Gosh, I looked at a ton of documents, and don't remember which ones," so be it.

Witnesses often ask the broader question "Should I study?" This question of whether or how much to review past documents, events, and so on will vary from case to case. Sometimes it's important to be familiar with the facts or documents to anticipate and rebut biased questions. Sometimes you risk re-creating inaccurate memory. Finally, sometimes it may be best to let sleeping (or forgotten) dogs lie. This is an important issue for you and your client to consider and discuss.

3. Review the Process

No matter how many episodes of their favorite legal TV show they've seen, and no matter how many times they've been a witness, don't make the mistake of assuming that witnesses really know—or understand—this bizarre process. Apologize, if you feel you must, for erring on the side of too much information, but then do precisely that—err, if at all, on the side of too much information.

Who, what, when, where, and why: every witness needs to hear and understand the basics.

> WHO: Who is involved in the litigation? Who will be there? Who will ask questions? Who will object? Who will see the testimony later? Who else may testify, and what will they say?
> WHAT: What happens when, and in what order? The oath? The questions? Which side begins? What should I bring? What should I wear?
> WHEN: When does the proceeding start and end? When are the breaks? When does the day end? When will I hear more about it?
> WHERE: Where will the proceeding take place? How do I get there? What type of place or room will it be?

WHY: What is the meaning, importance, and goal of this testimony—for each party concerned?

4. Put It Together

Understanding the facts and the process, how do you communicate effectively in a question-and-answer format? The facts do not change, but the method of answering questions is something that takes a lot of getting used to. Most of witness preparation, including the Ten Rules we will address in later chapters, is directed at this crucial part of the preparation.

Teach the client the unnatural and bizarre language of question and answer. Few clients realize how difficult *and* different this process is from everyday life. It is necessary to find creative ways to help them understand both points. One way is to minimize their defensiveness or embarrassment. I sometimes tell witnesses that I feel like their high school French (or Latin, or German) teacher who has to condense the whole school year into just a few hours. To teach how different this process is, I may talk about the difference between a lump of clay and a rock, explaining that most witnesses treat questions like clay: they work them, worry them, play with them, and often mold them into something else. I remind them that questions should be thought of like rocks—hard and fast words that should either be answered precisely as asked or challenged.

5. Anticipate Problems

Now is the time to identify things that may be seen as potential problems and prepare accordingly. Witnesses may have a wide range of concerns—large and small. Counsel has to ask about them and listen for them. For example, one commonly anticipated problem is nervousness: "How do I avoid being nervous?" "How will I be able to think clearly when I'm so nervous?" I give witnesses the same answer I give when I get the same question teaching trial practice to law students and lawyers: "Don't be nervous about being nervous. Everyone is nervous, and that's OK. You *should* be nervous: This is an important process."

Moreover, I *want* you to be nervous: it's the best way to sustain the kind of energy and intensity required to handle this process properly. So how does your witness overcome it? The best way is to stop worrying about the disease and just deal with the symptoms. Tell your client this: Don't worry about the fact that you're nervous; just think about what it is you do when you're nervous, and deal with that. For example, if you talk too fast when you're nervous, make an extra effort to slow down. Whatever it is, do the best you can, but don't worry about it.

Anticipate other potential problems and address these problems before testimony is given. Does your witness need a translator? Does the witness stutter? Does he or she need any special accommodations? What fears does the witness have about this process: do they involve the witness's job or reputation? Few clients *want* to be witnesses in legal proceedings, and a surprising number think their lawyer can wave a legal magic wand and make that obligation go away. Occasionally, there are ways to avoid questioning. But if not, there is much you can do to act as a buffer for your client before, during, and after questioning. Consider ways to control the timing, location, subject matter, or other elements, in addition to acting as the funnel or a shield from aggressive opposing counsel, investigators, or parties. This process is stressful enough for clients without allowing unnecessary intrusions.

Finally, prepare the witness for questions *about the preparation*! If the witness is a client, explain the attorney-client privilege, and that the questioner may ask about the logistics of preparation, but not what was communicated—orally or in writing. If the witness is *not* a client, make sure the absence of privilege is clearly understood so the witness is not caught by surprise. Moreover, make sure witnesses understand that your first, last, and fundamental message to them is always to tell the truth.

6. Do a Dry Run

Some years ago, I helped teach my twin girls to ride a bicycle, with all the scrapes and bruises and tears that came with that process. It was traumatic. Try as I might, I could not teach them to ride a bicycle by just talking to them; sooner or later, they had to try it themselves. All I could hope was to be there to help cushion the blow when they fell, and console and teach them after it happened. The same is true for teaching someone to be a better witness.

No amount of discussion can fully explain the question-and-answer process. Like anything difficult and unnatural, doing it right takes practice.

The best approach is to do a dry run, so your client can experience the process firsthand. It doesn't need to be formal or cover all the possible topics so long as it gives a clear sense of the process. However, the tougher and more realistic it is, the more helpful it will be to the client in the long run. I often have another lawyer in my office ask the questions, both to make it less awkward for everyone in role-playing and to allow me to show witnesses how I might act in representing them.

Do a dry run with every witness and you will be amazed at how productive it is. After you've gone through all the background information and reviewed the facts and the Ten Rules with them, they can now see the process in practice. Ideally, a dry run should be recorded in some fashion, if practical, and if covered by the privilege. This does not need to be any more elaborate or expensive than the case or client allows. Borrow a tape recorder or video camera. Find someone who works at home to type up the tape. It can be that simple.

Adapt the dry run to the proceeding. If you are preparing a witness for a deposition, you may want to have a transcript of the dry run prepared, since the goal of a deposition is to produce a clear and accurate transcript. This will emphasize the strengths and weaknesses of the testimony and will allow the witness to appreciate the final product and address any weaknesses. Most clients have never seen their spoken words in print. It's a revelation. If you're preparing someone for videotaped or live testimony, the transcript isn't quite as important, but the appearance is: the dry run may be videotaped. The important thing is to record the testimony in whichever way it will help you and your witness.

One other advantage of the dry run is to assess the witness's nonverbal communication, then help improve it. Go through it all and practice it: who she should look at (questioner, videographer, *not* you), how she is sitting (straight posture, avoiding distracting habits, and so on), what her body language is saying (relentlessly polite and positive), and what her body language is revealing (worried about this line of questioning, uncertain about the answer, and so on). At the same time, prepare her to *ignore* the questioner's body language; it's a distraction from the question itself.

7. Review Transcript

Another great benefit of doing a dry run is to generate and review a transcript or video. Depending on the case and the resources, this can mean anything from a full, videotaped session with a court reporter to a simple tape recording that can be typed up for review. If there are inaccuracies, it can prepare you and your client for the inevitable mistakes in any real transcript. Reviewing a videotape and/or transcript is the best way for both lawyer and client to see and understand how and why the rules set forth here work, and what your client can do better.

I believe that if you are working with a client, your mock transcript should not be discoverable in most jurisdictions. This is a privileged communication (and I always start the mock with a strong statement to that effect), conducted to explore issues and give advice in anticipation of litigation. I prepare witnesses to not talk about anything that happens in the preparation room, as it is privileged, and I jump fast to object if the questions violate that space. If the witness is not a client, then the answer is likely different, and I generally would *not* record the dry run.

The When and Where of Preparation

Lawyers and clients often ask how many days prior to the deposition preparation should occur? Should it occur as close to the date as possible, or should it be held a few days or weeks in advance to allow for follow-up questions by the witness? The answer is often both. Particularly in a complex case with many documents, events, issues, and so on, it's often good to meet one or more times well in advance, so there is time for follow-up review and questions (for both lawyer and client). However, the basic witness preparation must, to every extent possible, be in the days immediately before the testimony, or much of the impact will be lost.

The preparation time for a witness depends somewhat on the type of case and its subject matter. The more complex the case, and the more documents, events, issues, and so on that it involves, the more preparation time it will require. However, the basic process of helping someone understand the unnatural world of being a witness, including the rules, the mock procedure, and so on, requires an extensive and intensive commitment of time in *every* case. In addition, I always push hard to have both the preparation and the deposition take place away from my witness's place of business. The workplace holds too many distractions, mental and actual.

The witness environment is terribly unfair and deceptive: it has all the appearances of the questioner being in control. If the witness—and counsel—accept that deception, they have lost. This is, after all, the *witness's* testimony. True witness preparation is all about leveling the playing field, and helping the witness to take control.

Chapter 13

Basic Principles

There are two basic principles to follow when serving as a witness. Both principles seem obvious and simple, but they are actually quite complex and difficult. To present them as concepts is easy. To carry them out effectively as a witness requires a high level of understanding and discipline that can come only through preparation.

Principle 1: Listen, Listen, Listen

It has often been said that the three most important rules for being a witness are to listen, listen, listen. That is where the process begins, and it is the foundation for everything else. It is what we often think we do best, when it is actually an area where we fall short.

What most people worry about when they find out they are going to be a witness is talking: what will I say, how will I say it, and so on. Yet most people are able to say what's on their minds. They do it every day in conversation, and while they need to be prepared for how to say it in this new environment, the basic ability to speak is still there. What most people do *not* do in their normal lives is to *listen* with the kind of narrow intensity and precision required of a witness.

There are three basic reasons for this difference. For a witness, every word is: (1) taken down, (2) given great significance, and (3) intensely scrutinized. Thus, you must treat every word with this same extraordinary care, no matter who says it. In a normal conversation, if you don't listen carefully, it rarely matters! The conversation will keep going, even if it goes a little off track or becomes confusing. However, when every word has such significance, what is asked becomes part of the record. The words of the question become your witness's words, unless he or she says something to prevent it. The witness *must* listen carefully.

Part of the problem is that good listening in this context means focusing intensely and solely on the words that are spoken by the questioner. This is contrary to what we are used to. In the usual context, a good listener is someone who understands what the other person *means* to say or *wants* to say, not just the actual words spoken. A good conversationalist knows that the other person really means to ask what time it is, not just whether you know what time it is. A witness must tune out what the questioner might want to say or be trying to say and focus only on the actual words, in the same way that a transcript focuses only on the actual words. This is surprisingly hard to do with the necessary level of intensity and clarity.

The best way to achieve this kind of focus is to treat each question as if it were both the first and last one asked. Thinking of each question as the very first one will avoid the pitfalls of assuming context. In a normal conversation, if you say something once, you assume that the other person will put whatever else you say later in that context. A witness does not have that luxury: each question and answer will be examined and picked apart in isolation.

This out-of-context scrutiny has two key results. First, you have to put the prior questions out of your mind and listen only to the question at hand. Do not blend this question together with previous ones. Second, if there are facts or explanations that are essential to this answer that have already been asked, either clearly refer back to your previous testimony or restate the facts. It is not unusual in a testimony setting to have some repetition, and it is clearly not the fault of the witness. However many times a questioner chooses to bring up a subject, the answer remains the same. If the questions are repetitious—and they often are—then the answers must be repetitious.

Thinking of each question as the last one is even more important and more difficult than thinking of it as the first one. Too often, witnesses get caught up in guessing or trying to anticipate where the questioner is going, and as a result, they don't listen carefully enough to what is actually being asked. Consequently, the witness provides an answer that is not responsive to the question, and perhaps more troubling, it is an answer that opens up a line of questioning the examiner may not have been planning to pursue. Every good trial lawyer or investigator can tell stories about witnesses who were so intent on anticipating where the questions were going that they unknowingly pointed the questioner down a whole new and helpful path.

Remember, also, that *all* of the words of a question count. In this precise and artificial world, you ignore introductory or lead-in words of a question at your peril. For example:

Q: Isn't it true that after you found you were out of butter, then you went to the store?
A: Yes.

You may have focused on the key part of the question—going to the store. However, you have also adopted the questioner's assumption that you were out of butter, and by inference, why you went to the store. If all three assumptions are not completely correct, do *not* answer the question.

This is your statement and these are your words, so *you* should be in control. This includes controlling the pace, tone, and complexity of the questions. It includes, where necessary, questioning or challenging the questioner in pursuit of clear and fair questions.

A witness has every right to insist on that kind of fairness. The first big step toward that fairness is to listen with extraordinary intensity. Thus, you have the right to do what it takes to achieve that end. The Ten Rules set out in the following chapters are mechanical aids to help accomplish this.

Principle 2: Don't Try Too Hard

The second principle to follow when serving as a witness sounds simpler than the first, but it is actually even harder for most people to accomplish: don't try too hard. Most witnesses run into problems not because they are trying to lie but rather because they are trying too hard to tell the truth.

As White House counsel said to CJ on *The West Wing*, they are answering more than what was asked.

Much of what we do or say to keep a normal, casual conversation going must be avoided. In friendly conversation, to avoid looking rude, or foolish, or uninformed, or just to keep the conversation flowing, we often embellish or shade our knowledge or understanding in perfectly innocent and acceptable ways. We guess, we assume, we hide our lack of memory or knowledge, we gossip, we talk too much, and we speak without thinking carefully. Changing these conversational habits is hard work, but it is *essential* for successful testimony. It takes a surprising amount of preparation, concentration, and internal discipline.

The greatest challenge of being a witness is not making clear what you know but rather making clear what you *don't* know. This, again, is contrary to what we are used to in our everyday lives. The essence of being a good conversationalist is made up of two parts: first, to help the other person move the conversation along in interesting directions; and second, to be personable (or impressive). For a witness, neither of these is the priority.

A witness's goal is not to help anyone else do anything. It is only to be a truthful and efficient witness. Rather than moving anything forward, the goal is usually to be careful and precise, and then go home: to listen for simple questions, give simple answers, and then stop. This means that your words should be strictly limited. In general, as a witness you should talk only about what you absolutely remember: about what you *saw*, *heard*, or *did*. Anything more is going beyond what you truly know to be the truth and is trying too hard.

Think of any case, investigation, or dispute as a jigsaw puzzle. In one way or another, the questioner is trying to put the pieces together. He or she either wants to see what the overall picture on the top looks like, or (too often) wants it to fit his or her biased view of what it should look like. Meanwhile, inside that puzzle box is one small, strange-shaped piece that represents one witness's memory of what that witness *saw*, *heard*, or *did* on the matter. For a witness, the overall picture doesn't matter (or matters less). The witness's job is to define the limits of that one piece, and say "this far and no farther." It is to make clear, and keep clear, the precise size and shape of that one little piece. Failing to keep the lines clear or trying too hard can create conflicts with other witnesses or other evidence. Help your client understand that questioners *love* conflicts. They love to keep issues bubbling by creating conflicts—whether the conflicts are significant or not.

This creates a natural tension in every case between questioner and witness. The questioner will always want your piece of the puzzle to be larger, more flexible, and more consistent with his view of the overall picture. He will want you to know more, say more, and say it differently so he can solve the puzzle his way and do it with fewer pieces. Your job is to resist this natural tension and keep the lines clear between what you do and do not know.

One common outgrowth of this interaction is frustration for the questioner. An experienced questioner may exaggerate that frustration to try to bully more out of the witness. However, since that frustration is a predictable result, it should not come as a surprise, and it is not the witness's problem. Most investigators and questioners spend most of their lives feeling frustrated: it comes with the territory. Witnesses hardly ever give the questioner everything he or she wants, and the facts often do not support a questioner's suspicions.

Never let a questioner's expressions of frustration disturb you. Ignore them outwardly. Inwardly, you can take it as a good sign that you are exercising the kind of precision and control that a good witness should.

In keeping with the strange dynamics of being a witness, being boring is a good thing. This is a quest for *facts*, not for emotion or law. Be *factual*. If this is an investigation, deposition, or other preliminary stage, the more "interesting" you are, the more attractive you make yourself for the *next* round. Thus, although few witnesses want to go through the whole process a second or third time, the harder you try the first time, the more likely you make it that you will be brought back again.

Not trying too hard, thus being "boring," can also make you far less vulnerable on cross-examination or any other follow-up. The natural tendency to want to charm and please whoever is asking the questions ignores the fact that the other side will almost always have a chance to pick apart your answers. When that happens, your attempts at being helpful will be attacked as untruthful exaggerations. Do not fall into that trap. Don't try too hard.

Just as being a witness is not a test of your charm, it is also not a test of your intelligence. You will not be graded on how much you know, only on how accurate what you say is. You do not have to study the facts, unless your lawyer asks you to study the facts. You should *never* feel uncomfortable or defensive about what you don't know or don't remember, as long as the words you speak are precise and accurate.

Take a minute to understand just how hard this is to do. Think about how much pride we take in our intelligence and personality. What better place to demonstrate these qualities than in an important conversation like this, with important people listening? Doing anything else is awkward and uncomfortable because it is not natural. The more intelligent and outgoing the witness is by nature, the more inclined he or she will be to want to show off those qualities.

Remember, this is *not* a conversation. Being a witness involves the very difficult and constant discipline of putting these natural tendencies aside. Question, pause, answer, stop. Being precise and clear is tough, sometimes frustrating, work. Being an effective witness is not an easy process in the short run. Yet this discipline is essential to a witness's success in the long run and it increases the chances of getting through the process with the least damage and the highest likelihood of finality. The rules set out in the following chapters should help establish this discipline.

Chapter 14

Rule 1:
Take Your Time

If the old saying is true, that he who writes the rules wins the game, then the first rule for any witness is to take your time. This is the rule from which all else flows. Follow this, and the rest will be much easier. There are no shortcuts for a witness: The faster you try to go, the longer it will take; the harder you try to move things along and "be helpful," the more difficult it will be. It's all about multitasking and fairness.

Multitasking

As a witness, you cannot do everything that needs to be done to be effective, and also do it quickly: making sure you've heard the question clearly and understand it fully, considering it carefully, and formulating a clear and thoughtful answer. It's too much. This is not an environment in which you can think out loud, as we do all the time in our everyday lives. You have to carefully think through each step, and that can be done only if you take your time.

Fairness

Question, answer, question, answer. Like a volley in tennis, the faster it goes, back and forth, the sooner someone will make a mistake. But in tennis, that's fair: whoever makes the first mistake loses the point. In testimony, one of the players is invincible. If the questioner makes the first mistake, it doesn't matter: he or she is not under oath. If the witness makes the first mistake, it lives forever: under oath and duly recorded. What could be more grotesquely unfair? The first way to lessen that unfairness is to slow down: the slower, the fairer.

Every witness has the opportunity, the right, and the responsibility to control the pace of his or her testimony. No one else in the room is interested in slowing it down. If the witness doesn't do it, it won't happen. When I tell witnesses to slow down, I often get three reactions: First, "It's hard to do." Second, "It will look bad." Third, "It will make my testimony take longer." Let's look at all three concerns.

1. "It's hard to do."

Yes, it *is* hard to do. Normal conversation is fast-paced and free-flowing. We interrupt each other, finish each other's sentences, go where we think others want to go, all to make it fun and interesting. Yet all that is inappropriate and dangerous for a witness. Slowing down is uncomfortable and unnatural. To do it right, we have to do it mechanically.

Right from the *first question*, pause and silently count out a good five seconds after *every* question before answering. Don't wait until the middle of the testimony to do this—it will be much harder and you'll forget. Remember, it's *your* oath and *your* testimony: *You* should control the pace, whether it makes someone else happy or not. The written record looks the same whether you take a minute or a second to formulate your answer, but your answer will be better for the extra thought.

Pausing after *every* question will help you in several ways:

a. It will keep you from feeling rushed. People in a hurry make mistakes. Lawyers know that, and some may try to push you to go faster for that reason. If anyone questions your taking your time, you can very positively respond that you are just trying hard to tell the truth.

b. It will give you time to listen with the intensity and thought required to make sure you really understand the question. Among other things, it forces you to listen to the *entire question*. Too often in a normal conversation, we think we know where the conversation is headed, so we start our answer, or stop listening, before the other person has even finished the question. For a witness, this is confusing and even dangerous. The last words of the question may not be what you expected. Thus, you may be giving the wrong answer to what was asked, while at the same time answering a question that was not asked.

c. It allows you to be careful and disciplined enough to think about the best, most truthful, and most precise answer. Often the first thing that pops into your head is the *last* thing you want to have pop out of your mouth. The curse of the intelligent witness is that many people are used to thinking they know where the conversation is going and being in too much of a hurry to help it get there.

d. It will give your lawyer time to speak or object, if appropriate. If there is an objection, stop, listen, think about what is being said, and *wait* until you are advised to continue.

2. "It will look bad."

People sometimes worry that if they take their time, this will make a bad impression on the judge or jury. If it's a deposition, of course, we generally don't care what it looks like: the transcript is what matters. But it usually doesn't "look bad," regardless. Obviously, any of these rules can be taken to an extreme that becomes counterproductive, but it so rarely happens that I don't even like to discuss it with witnesses.

In my many years as a litigator, I have had many opposing lawyers complain that my witnesses were going too slowly, *but* I have *never* heard this from a juror or from a judge. Everyone else in the courtroom or hearing room understands how important the testimony is and that the importance of the testimony warrants the witness taking his or her time. As long as "taking your time" is done consistently, from the very first question, reasonably, and for the right reasons, then the witness should not worry about creating a bad impression.

Several years ago, I represented a contractor who was called to testify before a federal grand jury investigating a developer for fraudulent practices. When I met with him to prepare, it was clear that this rule was particularly important, because he liked to talk and talked too fast for a good witness. With preparation, he finally understood the significance of taking his time before responding. He went into the grand jury room, and since the lawyer for the witness is not allowed in a grand jury room, I had to wait outside. I didn't really know how successful he was going to be.

Sometime later, I was able to see a transcript of his testimony and, to my pleasant surprise, while reading the transcript, I could sense that he was going slowly and deliberately. It read like a transcript should: full questions, without interruption, and clear and careful answers. You could also sense the growing frustration of the questioner, who wasn't getting the snappy, sloppy, helpful answers that he wanted out of his witness. About an hour and a half into this three-hour testimony, the questioner said on the record, with obvious frustration, "I've noticed that you're pausing after each question. Is there a reason why you're doing something like that?" My witness responded (after a pause), "Because this is the most important thing I've ever done and I want to give you the most accurate answer that I possibly can." That was the end of that. All nonlawyers in a courtroom understand how important this is to the witness. Take your time.

3.   "It will make it take longer."

The first response is, "So what?" This is important: if it takes a little longer to do it properly, that is time well spent. The second response, though, is equally important. As in so many other ways, being a witness is unnatural and counterintuitive. In many situations, the reality is that the *slower* the witness goes, the *sooner* his or her deposition or other testimony will be over. Why? There are lots of reasons, but most often it is because the questioning lawyers really are not seeking deliberate and carefully considered responses to questions. They are fishing for the quick hit, the sound bite, the sloppy answer, the mistake. Once they realize they are facing a careful, disciplined witness, they lose interest. Time is money; there may be more productive places to fish. Or maybe they just start thinking of the pile of papers needing their attention back in their office. I have seen it happen time and again. The slower you go, the shorter your deposition will be. Take your time.

Taking control as a witness does not necessarily mean doing anything adversarial or unpleasant. On the contrary, you will generally want to avoid being too biased or one-sided. What it does mean is understanding that your role as a witness requires taking the time to make sure that you do it right, whether or not that results in a pace that someone else considers too slow. The first step toward taking control of your testimony is to take control of the pace. Take your time.

Chapter 15

Rule 2:
Always Remember You
Are Making a Record

One of the many unnatural things about being a witness is that often the most important person in the room is the only one who doesn't say anything: the person taking the notes. If it is formal testimony, that person may be a court reporter (or rather than a person, it may be a tape recorder). If it's a less formal interview, there will still be someone taking notes, and everyone should behave as if that person is a court reporter. Assume that everything—questions, answers, comments—is being taken down word for word.

As a federal prosecutor involved in organized crime and corruption cases, I reviewed thousands of pages of transcripts of secretly recorded tapes. These were either wiretaps, where none of the speakers knew they were being recorded, or consensual monitoring, where one of the participants, either an undercover agent or a cooperating witness, was recording the conversation. Those transcripts provided some important lessons for me in helping people create more formal transcripts as witnesses.

Keys to Testifying Successfully

First and foremost among the lessons I learned while reviewing transcripts is how careless we are in normal conversation: how we blur the lines between description and storytelling, between exaggeration and invention, between memory and guessing, and between vivid and inappropriate language. Why? Because it doesn't matter: it's all in fun, and no one will hold you to it tomorrow. Or will they? The court reporter is merciless. He or she is highly skilled in taking down every word as it is spoken, with no filtering or editing. Words spoken in haste in normal conversation may fade away just as quickly. But words spoken in haste to the court reporter are locked in forever.

Those words to the court reporter become the gift that keeps on giving. They are not just a problem then and there; they may come back again and again throughout the case. Moreover, they can come back in other cases, and in other circumstances. Those hasty words can cause years of harm to the speaker, as well as to the speaker's family, friends, colleagues, employer, and others. One has only to watch the news to see examples of this time and again.

What this means is that a witness cannot unring the bell. Once words come out of your mouth, they are committed to the cold written page, under oath. Even humor and sarcastic remarks read like factual statements in a transcript. Every word is there, for all to see, for all time.

What is the best way for a witness to confront this reality? One key to testifying successfully is to take your time. Another is to consider choice of language very carefully.

Take Your Time

First, slow down and be precise. Answer each question as if you were dictating the first and only draft of an important document. (*You are!*) Consider each word carefully. This is extremely difficult to do. I have used a dictating machine for many years for all kinds of documents and have become very good at it. Yet even with all that experience, I am still constantly rewinding, rethinking, rewording, and retaping. Then, even after that process, nothing I dictate actually goes out unless I have also reviewed (and usually edited) the printed copy! A witness has none of these advantages, yet *your* dictated document (unlike most of mine) is under oath.

Try this exercise: Get a tape recorder or dictating machine. Think about an important and upsetting event in your life from over a year ago, not related to whatever it is you are being asked to be a witness about. Sit down in a quiet place, turn the machine on, and describe what happened from start to finish, without stopping either your description or the tape. Then put the tape away, or better yet, give it to someone who can type it up for you. Most people have rarely seen their spoken words in print. At least a day later, listen to the tape or read the transcript. You will be amazed at how much you missed, and how much you would now do differently. If you then consider the added difficulty of listening and responding to a stranger's questions, you will get some sense of how difficult this process is.

We will discuss some of the basic rules for being careful and precise later, but it may be helpful here to think about some common issues that can create problems on the record:

- Talk in complete sentences. Unless it is a *very* clear and simple question, the questions should not be answered yes or no. Beware of compound questions, or questions with double negatives in them.
- In discussing conversations, make it clear whether you are paraphrasing or quoting directly. Don't put words in someone else's mouth unless you are 100 percent sure of them.
- Do not adopt a questioner's summary of your prior statements. The questioner may give a summary that is true but incomplete or distorted. If so, just answer no, and if you are asked why you answered no, you can explain or elaborate.

A document this important cannot be dictated quickly, casually, or off the cuff. You need to be fully prepared, and then approach it with the right sense of pace, care, and precision.

Be Conscious of Language

Second, be aware of the power of language. In a casual conversation, we are very relaxed, even sloppy, about language and choice of words. When every word is transcribed and under oath, language takes on an extraordinary importance, far beyond normal conversation. Then, when two or more sides are fighting over what those words mean, and each side is trying to use them for its own purposes, the problems multiply. We must be aware of, and carefully consider, each word in the question.

There are five basic language issues that witnesses must confront and be prepared for:

1. Confusing Language
2. Jargon
3. Legalese
4. Relative Language
5. Loaded Language

Some of these obviously overlap, but it is worth considering each one separately.

1. Confusing Language

Open a dictionary at random to any page, and you will see a basic truth: there are very few simple words; most have more than one meaning. In the heat of litigation, those differences can be blown up in degree and significance. If the witness is not 100 percent clear about how the questioner is using a word, the witness *cannot* answer the question. Otherwise, the questioner will assume that his or her own definition is the one in play.

I talked about this issue of different meanings at a CLE program years ago, and someone came up to me at the break and said, "As an example, you should talk about contranyms." A contranym, I discovered, is a word that can have two opposite meanings. For example:

- *Buckle*: to hold together or to fall apart;
- *Clip*: to cut off or to attach;
- *Oversight*: to watch carefully or to miss completely.

Certainly, these specific words may never come up, but it is a dramatic reminder that words can have very different meanings.

One common tactic is for a questioner to try to bully his way through language problems. Consider this exchange:

Q: Whom did you report to?

A: Please rephrase the question.

Q: What don't you understand about my question?

A: I'm not comfortable with "report." I had consultants and investors, but "report" sounds like I'm in the army.

Q: You know what the word "report" means, don't you?

A: Well, yeah.

The witness gave in to a question with the unspoken "you idiot!" at the end. But when I spoke to her later, I told her that the issue was not whether she was too stupid to know what "report" means (which was how she felt it). The issue was whether the questioner was too stupid to know that the dictionary has 25 different definitions of the word, and she didn't know which one was meant! Be sure you know *before* you answer.

Take another example: a simple word like "fall." Webster's Dictionary defines it as "to descend freely by the force of gravity." When they were younger, my twin girls had bunk beds. To them, rolling out of the bottom bunk was not a "fall"—it was just rolling out of bed. But even to them, rolling out of the top bunk was "to descend freely by the force of gravity." So there was a small railing on the top bunk to prevent a "fall."

I have been called in by several health-care companies that are involved with nursing homes, to help their trial counsel prepare executives and others for deposition and trial testimony. In the nursing home world, there is a great deal of discussion of falls: fall reporting, fall statistics, fall prevention programs, fall risk levels, and so on. Imagine the impact of all this on Juror #6; he hears the word "fall," and at least part of him is thinking "top bunk." Why is Grandma "descending freely by the force of gravity?" How can the nursing home let this happen? Opposing counsel can take advantage of this by using that simple word as a weapon.

But words have different meanings in different contexts, and in the nursing home world, that's not what "fall" means. In that context, it simply means "found on the floor" (*CMS State Operations Manual*, § 483.25(h)). Thus, if a resident is "found on the floor," and no one saw how she got there—even if she is happy and unhurt, and may just have sat down—that is a federally reportable fall, and the nursing home is required to record and respond. The witness knows this; Juror #6 does not. It is up to the witness (and counsel) to make sure that the correct meaning is made clear.

2. Jargon Language

Every profession, industry, and region, and any number of other categories, has its own language. We call it jargon. In Webster's words, jargon is "the technical terminology or characteristic idiom of a special activity or group."[1] But like so many other words, jargon has multiple meanings. When Juror #6 hears jargon, it comes across less as impressive technical know-how, and more like Webster's *next* definition of the word: "obscure and often pretentious language marked by circumlocutions and long words." Witnesses need to work hard to stay away from jargon, and to recognize when they fall back into it, and stop to explain.

Consider one small example (actual, but modified for confidentiality). In the introductory minutes of a lengthy deposition, the following exchange took place:

Q: What management position did you hold?
A: I was responsible for all the R&D projects for BASU for filler metals.

A tripleheader! In one short answer, of roughly 13 words, three impenetrable pieces of jargon: "R&D projects," "BASU," and "filler metals." The witness apparently thinks he's given his job description. In fact, what he's given Juror #6 is nothing, except perhaps the lingering perception that this guy is a jerk.

Jargon interferes with communication in so many ways. Jurors don't understand it. They don't like it and often feel it's condescending. It can make the witness seem cold and distant: talking about human issues in dehumanizing terms. In fact, though, we badly understate the problem if we just say that jargon interferes with communication. If you look at it from the perspective of Juror #6, it is far worse. It forces Juror #6 into three bad choices. If a witness uses jargon, Juror #6 can only:

---

1. Merriam-Webster.org.

1. ignore it, which defeats the lawyer's purpose in having the witness say it;
2. spend the next several minutes trying to figure it out, in which case the testimony that follows is lost; or
3. decide the witness is a jerk, and ignore *everything* the witness says.

Any of these choices can be damaging to the witness, and to the case. Help your witness to understand what kind of jargon he or she speaks, and how to avoid it.

Jargon makes a witness appear distant when it overwhelms the reality of the moment. One common example comes in medical malpractice cases. Medicine cannot do everything. There will always be bad results, and some patients will die. No matter how good the medical care may have been, it's hard for many doctors and other providers to talk about patients who don't get better. There will always be lingering self-doubt and regret. When forced to answer questions about these difficult matters, many doctors and other professionals try too hard to treat an emotional subject rationally.

In trying to be rational, the witness quickly retreats into medical jargon. That may be fine in a medical journal analysis or a peer review, but it is not what laypeople want to hear. The harder the questions become, the greater the retreat into jargon. Slowly but surely, a caring health professional comes across as a cold, distant technician. It is more comfortable for many witnesses to seek refuge in jargon, but it can have a devastating impact on the witness's credibility and sympathy. Plain, emotional English would be a more truthful reflection of how you feel and a better way to reach out and persuade the listener.

Jargon can also make a witness's words confusing to outsiders. A statement that cannot be understood is of no use. I once represented a group of top scientists in testimony before the Nuclear Regulatory Commission. In part because the investigating agency is quasi-scientific, many of the scientists were tempted early and often to speak technically. However, the eventual audience was made up of some nonscientists, and back-and-forth jargon ran the risk of making the testimony so confusing that it would be almost useless without a science jargon interpreter.

The quick resort to jargon can also be dangerous for the witness. Some years ago, I prosecuted a case involving a fatal industrial accident. On direct examination, one of the defense's expert witnesses gave a presentation that was so filled with jargon that while somewhat confusing, it seemed to show an impressive knowledge of the subject.

However, the more I pressed on cross-examination, the clearer it became that there was no depth to his knowledge. He could give a technical-sounding opinion, but then could not explain or defend it. He knew the words, but not what was behind them. The clearer it became how limited his knowledge was, the more he retreated into jargon, and the more meaningless the jargon became. By trying to sound more familiar with the subject than he really was, he ended up coming across as dishonest to the jury.

Don't make these mistakes. Speak clearly and plainly. If you must use jargon, stop immediately to explain it. Remember, the point is to communicate, not to impress. Keep it simple.

3. Legalese

Every case has legal standards and concepts that must be broken down from their confusing language and explained in clear and simple terms. Counsel must help the witness understand what they are, so they don't stumble upon them blindly—or get lured into them unsuspectingly. Then witness and counsel must be ready to deal with them during testimony.

The greatest language challenges come when a word exists in the intersection of two or three language worlds—that is, when a word has different meanings in English, jargon, and/or legalese. Then, it is particularly important for the witness to be 100 percent sure which meaning the questioner intended, or he or she cannot answer the question.

Two quick examples follow. The first involves the seemingly innocuous word "manage" and the related "manager." In English it can mean a range of things: from managing a sports team (where "manager" and "coach" can be either synonymous, or very different roles), to managing a checkbook, to managing to escape a dull party. In the jargon of some businesses and industries, "manager" has a particular meaning—which may or may not mean the real "boss." In legalese, many state legislatures, in their wisdom, gave the corporate secretary of an LLC the name "manager," even though such a statutory manager may be there only to sign documents, and may have little or nothing to do with running the business. Which meaning does the questioner mean?

Another example is "standard of care." Seems like a simple phrase, and many unprepared witnesses assume that it means whatever is logically the right way to do something. It could pertain to the way they were trained, or something in a book, or just something that makes sense. But "standard of care" in a legal proceeding has a very different—and *far* more limited—legal definition. Different jurisdictions phrase it differently, but the best and simplest definition is just five words: "reasonable care under the circumstances." It's a phrase bookended by two words that clearly *remove* it from the realm of books or fixed standards: what were the "circumstances" at the time, and given all that, what was "reasonable" for that person or entity to do? Common usage or legalese—which meaning does the questioner mean?

If you're not 110 percent sure what the questioner meant by a word or a phrase, do not answer the question. Remember the most important person: the court reporter. He or she doesn't know what the word means, or which meaning is intended, unless either the questioner or the witness makes it clear. Insist on the discipline of clarity.

4. Relative Language

"Did you have those important meetings frequently?" The words seem simple and common enough, but something is wrong. Simple does not mean clear, and common does not mean precise. A witness needs both clarity and precision. Relative terms are words that ask the witness to place something on a continuum, with no reference points. They almost guarantee that the questions and witness will view the word, and the testimony, differently.

Examples of relative language include the following:

- frequently
- substantial
- common
- normal
- general (or in general)
- important
- regular

These are words for which—to get clarity and precision—the response would have to be: "Compared to what?" Were these meetings "important"? Compared to what? Other meetings? Which ones? When? With whom? Were these meetings "frequent"? Compared to what? Hourly events? Daily? Monthly? Quarterly?

The problem is that the questioner may mean one thing by the word, but the witness means something very different. The questioner—now or later—will try to use that gap to her advantage. Don't let her. Just say, "Please rephrase the question."

5. Loaded Language

"It's not what you say, it's how you say it." Loaded words are those that seek to have an emotional impact—positive or negative. In every case, there are at least two kinds of loaded words: those that counsel putting on a witness *want* that witness to use, and those that they do *not* want them to use. Part of preparation is helping the witness to sort out which is which, and be ready for both. Think about the different ways a witness could describe the same thing. For example:

The car *flew* through the stop sign.	The car *went past* the sign.
The car *smashed* into the bus.	The car *brushed* the side of the bus.
The children were *screaming* in panic.	The children were *upset*.

If the question contains loaded language the witness doesn't agree with, don't answer it. But that process must start in preparation. Always remember, the most important person in the room may be the court reporter, and—regardless—language *matters*.

Chapter 16

Rule 3: Tell the Truth

No witness takes an oath simply to tell the truth. That is a myth. The oath at the beginning of testimony is to tell "the truth, the whole truth, and nothing but the truth." Like many things in our normal lives, we tend to blur it all together into one image. Like many things in the precise and artificial world of being a witness, we need to examine the *entire* statement and make sure that we understand and consider all three parts. There are, after all, three parts to the oath for good reasons.

1. The Truth

Witnesses should understand that this is not only a rule of law, it is a rule of self-preservation. Lying or stretching the truth on the witness stand may not only be a crime, it's foolish. Assume that the questioner is more experienced than you think, and that his or her experience includes the ability to make a witness who is playing fast and loose with the truth very uncomfortable.

If a questioner suspects that you are not being honest, he or she can take a variety of approaches to try to catch you in a lie. The consequences of telling a lie are often worse than whatever it was the questioner was asking about in the first place. It is what we used to call the Watergate Syndrome and more recently have referred to as the Martha Stewart Syndrome: people getting caught and prosecuted for covering up, not for the initial subject matter being investigated. Don't do it. Tell the truth.

"Oh, What the Heck!"

As the questioning drags on, as you are asked about the same things over and over, as the questioner makes clear that he or she doesn't like or doesn't believe your version, there is a natural (and understandable) tendency to say, "Oh, what the heck," and give them a little more of what they seem to want. After all, maybe the question is only slightly wrong, maybe someone else could see it that way, and maybe if you give them what they want, they will finally move on to something else.

Unfortunately, all three of these maybes are misguided and dangerous for a witness. First, when you are under oath and every word will be taken down and picked apart, there is no such thing as "slightly wrong." If something is not completely and precisely true, don't say it (or agree with it); it will only cause you more problems. Second, it doesn't matter what someone else's view of the matter might be, or whether that view is or isn't reasonable. That mysterious "other person" is not the witness. You are. Finally, if you give them what they want, they will not go away. They will only want more.

There are no shortcuts here. What is true in mathematics is equally true in this process: "the shortest distance between two points is a straight line." The truth of what you saw, heard, or did, and remember, is a narrow, precise line. No matter how often or how hard someone tries to get you to veer off that line, resist the "Oh, what the heck" tendency. Once you're off track, it becomes harder and harder to get back on. No matter how many times a question is asked, and in however many different ways, the truth—and your truthful answer—must remain the same. Your best intentions to help "move things along" will only slow them down, because you will spend time trying to end the detour and get back on that straight line.

Mistakes

Everyone accepts the old maxim "nobody's perfect." Yet, in a witness environment, many people tend to forget that. The setting, the oath, and the court reporter all combine to make them feel that they must not make a mistake. They feel like someone is grading them, and any mistake will hurt their grade. So, when they inevitably make a mistake, they panic, and either ignore it or try to mold and shape it—like clay—into something else. Don't do it: when you make a mistake, which every witness does at some point, keep two things in mind.

First, remember the Law of Holes: "When you're in a hole, stop digging!" Trying to work around a mistake will ultimately only make it worse. As soon as you realize you made a mistake—however that happens: on your own, because you hear it come back at you in another question, or in some other way—stop and fix it. There are lots of ways to do this, but one of the easiest and most effective is the simple word "clarify." The goal is a clear and accurate record, so stop and clarify any mistakes. You can clarify anything, such as:

- something you remembered wrong;
- something you were confused about;
- a poor choice of words (by you or the questioner); and
- an incomplete or distorted answer.

Second, don't worry about it. This is *not* school, you are *not* being graded, and you should *not* expect to be perfect. More importantly, Juror #6 doesn't expect you to be perfect either. He's nervous, too. He knows that he would make mistakes, and he does not want robots talking to him. Your mistake draws you closer to him, not further away. If you make an honest mistake, and honestly try to clarify it, any attempt by the questioner to cut you off, or make much ado about nothing, should reflect badly on him or her, not on you.

My favorite quote about mistakes is by Elbert Hubbard, from *The Notebook*: (1927) "The greatest mistake you can make in life is to be continually fearing you will make one." It can be critical to a witness's success for the preparation process to take away some of that fear of making mistakes.

2. The Whole Truth

The whole truth means both the good stuff and the bad stuff. Both need to come out, and in many situations, the witness must take the lead in bringing them forward.

The Bad Stuff

None of us is perfect, and most of us have things in our past that are embarrassing or difficult. The Internet, and its search engines, can make those things live forever. For a witness, some of those things may become relevant, or the questioner will try to make them relevant. The key is to avoid making the situation worse by trying to hide or be defensive about these things. As prosecutors, we used the acronym BOBS: bring out the bad stuff. Whatever the issues are, you and your lawyer can deal with them. It will be much harder if they come out only after you've tried to cover up or gloss over the problems.

Be open and honest with your lawyer beforehand, and be prepared to bring out the bad stuff directly and openly. This will take away from the questioner the opportunity to make you look bad (and to make the problems look worse) by having to drag it out of you.

Here's an example that is extreme but instructive. Years ago, as a federal prosecutor with the Organized Crime Strike Force, I prosecuted a large drug-smuggling and corruption case in Georgia. Like many complex business ventures, this criminal operation needed a "broker" to bring together the different players: importers, pilots, landing-strip people, corrupt cops, truckers, distributors, and so on. That broker was a man we'll call Bobby, who had done this successfully for years. However, when Bobby was caught in the middle of a dispute between people he had brokered in an unrelated deal and they came after him with guns blazing (literally), he decided that it would be a good time to switch sides and become a witness for the government.

When I first met with Bobby to begin preparing for his testimony, it was clear there was a problem. Bobby was a very proud man—proud of his criminal accomplishments and proud of his decision to become (in his view) God's gift to law enforcement. After his long life of crime, the image he had of himself as Bobby the Great Law Enforcer was not real; it would open him up to damaging cross-examination and would turn off the jury. Over several days of working together, we kept coming back to my insisting that he be candid about his prior crimes, instead of fulfilling his desire to be the good guy. Finally, he looked at me, sighed heavily, and said, "You want me to be a bad guy, don't you?" We were getting somewhere.

As a result, throughout several days of testimony at trial, Bobby was a great witness. He was open and honest about his criminal past. The jury was horrified, but more importantly, they believed him: this was clearly the real Bobby. They hung on his every word. One after another, the defense lawyers got nowhere with him on cross-examination. There was nowhere to go: he hadn't hidden or glossed over anything and having him repeat what he had already said only made him more believable.

The last defense lawyer to cross-examine Bobby got so frustrated that, as a final rhetorical "question," he bellowed, "In fact, you haven't had an honest job in 20 years!" He then threw his pencil on the table and sat down. Of course, it was a dramatic flourish, not a question, and no one expected an answer. No one except Bobby, who remembered from his preparation to listen carefully to each question, pause, then answer it truthfully and simply. Question, pause, answer, stop. He listened, thought awhile, and then in a firm, clear voice said, "Actually, I think it's 21 years!" The courtroom burst out in laughter, the point of making him out to be a bad guy was lost, and Bobby walked off the witness stand an honest crook. Sixteen people, including two former county sheriffs, were convicted in the case.

No matter what the problem is, no matter how large or small, it is *always* better to talk about it and prepare for it beforehand, and bring it out willingly in testimony. Don't give the questioner a gift he doesn't deserve by adding the claim that you tried to cover it up.

Be Yourself

Too often, witnesses try to pretend that they are someone different from their true selves. The reality is that questioners, judges, and juries are often pretty good at spotting a phony; once they think they've found one, that witness's credibility goes out the window.

All of us are uneven. We are better at some things than others. The problem is that we don't like to accept, or admit, those differences. Yet they are all part of the truth of who we are. In private practice, I defended a doctor who was charged with criminal tax evasion, having failed to report and pay taxes on a large amount of money over a three-year period. There was no question that her tax returns were wrong; our defense was that it was not intentional.

As a professional, my client was extraordinarily intelligent, qualified, and articulate. She had testified in court on other cases as an expert witness. Unfortunately, as talented as she was in her work, she was equally untalented in her personal life. Her finances and record keeping were a terrible mess, and she was justifiably embarrassed. In her defense, we had to show that part of her life to be the disaster it truly was, and to do that, we needed her to testify.

A life of being the competent, confident expert made what would have been difficult for anyone sheer torture for her. She wanted to explain the mess, justify it, minimize it, blame others for it, anything not to look that bad in public. It took a long time to convince her that all of that was phony, not who she really was. If the gap between what she did well and what she did badly was unusually large, that made her task as a witness more difficult, but it was not one that she could avoid.

In the end, she understood. She testified about how her disorganized finances had been a chronic problem and a constant source of embarrassment. Outside factors may have made things worse, but only because she was in such bad shape to begin with and hadn't changed. It was difficult, but it was clearly honest. After she was acquitted, the judge gave her a strong lecture on her need to get a good bookkeeper. Everyone agreed.

In many ways, large and small, telling the truth means being yourself. That does not mean that you shouldn't work hard in preparation to be careful and precise in expressing yourself. It just means that you cannot be a precise phony.

The Good Stuff

Just as witnesses must take responsibility for bringing out the bad stuff, they must also bring out the good stuff about themselves, their work, those involved in the litigation, and other matters. The questioner will not ask: it must come from the witness. For example, I have worked with a wide range of health-care professionals. They get up in the morning, get dressed, have some breakfast, go to work—and then spend the day saving lives, or helping those in need. After a while, to them, it's just what they do every day, nothing special to talk about. But to Juror #6, it is amazing, wonderful work, if it's truthfully described.

That can come only from the witness. Every witness, in every profession and in all walks of life, has good stuff to talk about. An important goal of preparation is to find it, and convince the witness that for this one day it is not vanity to talk about it. It is an essential part of telling the whole truth.

In a deposition, if the witness does not bring out the good stuff—and the best parts of your case—during the other side's questioning, you can and should consider doing a direct of your own at the end. That creates good material that can be used at various points down the road. Even at trial, if the other side designates portions of the deposition to read or show to the jury, many jurisdictions will allow counsel to cross-designate the good stuff from direct.

3. Nothing but the Truth

In this environment, truth has a different and more precise meaning than it does in a normal conversation. Truth in a conversation is what you believe. If I believe that something is true, I'm not lying by talking about it. But "belief" includes guesses, inferences, and all kinds of other things that stretch a precise definition of the truth. Truth in the witness environment is strictly limited to what the witness *saw, heard,* or *did.* Anything beyond that is speculation. If you try to have a normal conversation in which all you say is what you saw, heard, or did, it will be almost impossible. This is not the type of interaction that we pride ourselves on as conversationalists, but this is the truth in the precise and narrow sense that is used here.

Thus, a witness can testify to something if the witness "saw" it—that is, witnessed it or read it; "heard" it—that is, heard someone say it, whether to the witness or others; or "did" it—that is, wrote it, said it, or took some other action. Everything else is a guess. So much of what makes us intelligent, interesting, intuitive people, and so much of what makes us good conversationalists, is based on our view of what's in someone else's head. Why did someone do something? What did they mean when they said something? How did they react to something or someone? It's all guessing. We do it every day in normal conversation, and we take pride in it. But don't do it as a witness.

Telling the truth, the whole truth, and nothing but the truth is hard work, but it is essential.

Chapter 17

Rule 4: Be Relentlessly Polite

Don't tell witnesses to be polite; tell them to be relentlessly polite—and relentlessly positive. This is not etiquette advice. It's a survival technique.

Being polite in this environment can be a tough, often thankless, job, but it is one that is essential to being a good witness. It's hard work, but it's necessary. The experience of being a witness can run the whole gamut from a polite, friendly session to an angry, adversarial one. Some matters are more emotional than others, and some questioners are more confrontational than others. With all the different factors that may influence how the questioning goes, it's often hard to predict whether you may experience these kinds of problems.

It doesn't matter. Whatever the tone of the questioner or the questions, your response should always be the same: coolly, unflappably, relentlessly, even infuriatingly, polite and positive. Start that way at the beginning, and do not change until it's over. It's all about understanding the *audience* and the *challenge*.

The Audience

As discussed earlier, we spend a lifetime talking to the people who are talking to us. It's the natural thing to do. But one of the hardest adjustments to this very *un*natural witness environment is understanding that that is not what's happening here. The lawyer is generally *not* the main audience: it's the judge, jury, or other finder of fact. So, arguing with or getting angry with the lawyer will only interfere with your communicating with the real audience.

The Challenge

This is not a game. Your job as a witness is not to score points or make points. Rather, your job is to listen hard, think carefully, and answer questions if you can. Anything else is just an unnecessary distraction, which will only diminish your credibility. All good questioners know that an upset witness is an unfocused witness, so if they can throw in a little sarcasm, a garbage question or two, or "three teaspoonfuls of righteous indignation," why not? Any antagonism is often just an act to get you flustered. Do not let it happen.

Be Positive

This is your testimony. Be proud of it—all of it! Say it positively. Yes, I did that! Yes, I wrote that! Don't let a lawyer adopting an aggressive or accusatory stance influence your attitude. If a witness *sounds* negative or defensive, those who listen will assume that he or she has something to be negative or defensive *about*. Don't make that mistake. Regardless of the substance—good or bad—remain positive.

Be Relentlessly Polite

Being "relentlessly polite" includes being relentless: both counsel and the *witness* must prepare to *never* let the witness be interrupted. Whether it's accidental or intentional, the witness should never allow opposing counsel to interrupt. It's the witness's testimony. Just pause, and then politely but firmly say, "I'm sorry, I wasn't finished with my answer. I need to finish it, then I'll answer your next question." Then finish your answer—but really finish it! Some witnesses will shorten their answers when interrupted. No. Answer fully and with gusto, and you may find that you get fewer interruptions. If interruptions become a real problem, then counsel should intervene by objecting and by asking, either right then or on cross, for you as the witness to finish your answer.

Keep Your Cool

Being a witness is a surprisingly emotional experience. Why? Most people are used to others being positive, pleasant, and, if all else fails, diplomatic.

Suddenly, in front of strangers, in a strange environment, witnesses are under attack. Their work, profession, company, competence, credibility, decision-making ability, friends, family, and more are fair game. Keep your cool. No lawyer's question changes reality. You are the same good person, trying to do your best, that you were before you began. Be positive. Stand your ground. But do it politely and persuasively. Anger rarely persuades.

Don't Tease the Bear

Everyone here has a job to do; the questioner's job is to ask questions. Do not waste your time and energy belittling or attacking the questioner's job, or thinking, saying, or implying negative things about the matter or investigation, the questions, or anything else. You will accomplish nothing, you will distract yourself from *your* difficult job, and you will needlessly antagonize the questioner. If the questioner is the government, that makes unnecessary antagonism particularly pointless—and foolish.

Leave It to the Lawyers

Your lawyer is there to be both your advisor and, to some extent, your buffer or protector. If there is a reason for things to get difficult, leave that to your lawyer. Stay above the fray. Your lawyer can give and take the heat without it reflecting directly on you.

Meanwhile, if there are discussions, objections, or arguments among counsel, take the opportunity to listen and learn: What are the issues and problems, and how can you best handle them in your answers? After *any* discussion or distraction, take the opportunity to ask for the question again, so that you can listen to it without disruption and with the benefit of having heard the preceding debate.

Don't Play Games

This could also come under Rule 3, Tell the Truth. Keep it simple, clear, and direct. Thinking that you can avoid the tough questions by dancing or fencing with the questioner is arrogant nonsense. Dodging and weaving will only make you look like you are hiding something, and will goad the questioner on to more and tougher questions. If you can't give direct, truthful answers to direct questions, don't say anything. Playing games will only make it worse.

Common witness games include:

The Tense Game: "Ask about yesterday, I'll tell you about today; ask me about today, I'll tell you about tomorrow." We were given an example of this at the highest level of government when President Clinton gave his first television interview responding to claims that he had had an affair with a White House intern. No one claimed the affair was still going on: the question was whether it had ever happened. Yet Clinton repeatedly dodged that question by responding only in the present tense that "there *is* no" affair. Although in later statements his denials became clearer, that initial dodge left a sense of dishonesty that was hard to dispel.

The Definition Game: "You may think it means this, but I think it means that." Once again, President Clinton gave us an example. Asked a question about an "affair" with the young woman, he responded that there was no "improper relationship." Asked what that meant, he gave no definition. That may work in a brief sound bite or press conference. Under the glare and repeated questioning of real testimony, this game leads only to trouble.

The Dodge Game: "You ask me about this, I'll tell you about that." This involves simply dodging the question asked, and answering an unasked question instead. In the hands of a skilled questioner, engaging in this game, like the other games, will only make your life as a witness miserable.

All of these games have been tried before. None of them work in the long run. Benefit from the bad experiences of prior game players: Don't try it. Just answer the question.

Don't Get Spooked by Details

Many questioners thrive on endless, meaningless details. There are lots of reasons for this. Sometimes it has just become part of their routine. For example, the Securities and Exchange Commission (SEC) in its internal manual for conducting investigations has a standard script for all cases, which contains an absurd number of detailed background questions: everything from your Social Security number to your home phone number (even when your lawyer is sitting right there and the SEC knows it would be improper for them to call you directly). Because it's in the script, SEC investigators ask these questions of all kinds of witnesses in all kinds of cases, even when there's absolutely no reason to go into that kind of detail.

Sometimes the reasons are not just bureaucratic. Perhaps the questioner is just flexing his or her muscle by asking seemingly prying questions to emphasize having the power to ask, or to try to intimidate you. Don't let the questioner win that game. Most of the time, the questioner has wide berth to ask background questions. Even if a question is questionable, often it's not worth the time and expense to try to block the questioner's ability to ask it. Unless your lawyer objects, don't worry about it. Just answer the questions.

Take the Questioner's Frustration as a Compliment

Years ago, I went to my son's first football game. He played defensive line, did well, his team won, and I prepared to congratulate him as they came off the field at the end. But to my surprise, he was very upset. I asked why. "It's not fair," he said, "They kept putting two guys on me, and I couldn't get to the quarterback!" I smiled and said, "Use your math. Both sides only have 11 guys. If they have to put two on you, what does that mean?" He looked a little less upset, and replied, "It means they have one less to stop everyone else?" "Yes, it means you're doing something right: use their frustration as a compliment," I told him. "If they put two guys on you, think to yourself, 'Thanks for the compliment; now get out of my way!'"

The same thing applies for witnesses. A prepared and disciplined witness can be *very* frustrating to an unprepared lawyer. Witnesses often assume that the questioner's frustration means they've done something wrong. No! More often than not, the questioner's frustration means the witness is doing something *right*! Don't change. Take that frustration as a compliment. If you were doing something that helped your testimony, keep doing it—and more! You are there to give the truth, the whole truth, and nothing but the truth—not to fulfill the questioner's fantasies.

If you are going to be able to truly "listen, listen, listen," you need to avoid anything that will make that unnatural discipline even more difficult. To accomplish this, you need to keep your cool throughout the process. The more careful and precise you are in listening and answering, the more frustrated the questioner may become. Remember, though, that nothing the questioner says is evidence unless you agree to it. Their frustration—whether real or exaggerated—should not push you to agree. Anger and argument will interfere with the work you have to do, so don't play that game. Instead, be relentlessly polite.

Chapter 18

Rule 5: Don't Answer a Question You Don't Understand!

In the futuristic movie *I Robot*, a detective played by Will Smith speaks to a computer-generated hologram of a dead scientist. When the detective's questions veer off from being clear and simple, the hologram intones, "I'm sorry, my responses are limited; you must ask the right questions!" Real witnesses, even more than holograms, have both a right and a responsibility to insist on clear and fair questions.

In a casual conversation, it's common for one person not to understand fully or with certainty what another is asking, but it's also unimportant. The conversation flows along in a new direction, and if the person who asked the question cares, he or she can bring it back by asking the question again, or in some other form. You would never be so blunt as to simply say, "Please rephrase the question," and stop. Precision is not the point, and if it gets in the way of the conversation's flow, it loses every time.

By contrast, in the unnatural environment of being a witness, precision is crucial. When everything that's said is being taken down and picked apart, the question becomes part of the answer. When you answer a question, it will be assumed that you understood the question and that you agree with anything in the question that you do not clearly dispute. If you later get a chance to review a transcript, you will be amazed at how many questions were really unclear or misunderstood. However, by the time you read the transcript, it's too late.

The key here again is taking control. You are the witness; this is your statement. You have a right to clear, simple questions and to answer only questions you understand. Otherwise, *don't answer*. Just say, "Please rephrase the question," and stop. Do no more than that. There is no limit to how many times you can ask until you get a question you understand. Do not offer to get into a discussion over what you did not understand and don't help the questioner by saying, "Do you mean X or do you mean Y?" He or she may have meant Z, something entirely different, but now you'll be asked all three questions! The only exception here is if the question is clear but the context is not: What time frame are we talking about? Which person are we talking about? What location are we talking about? In these types of instances, it may be reasonable (depending on what you and your lawyer agree upon) to ask for the context, not just a rephrasing.

A dirty little secret of the legal profession is that this discipline to say, "Please rephrase the question" really works. Witnesses complain to me all the time, "That is not going to work. He is just going to ask the same question again." But even if he does, so what? What has the witness lost? However, in an extraordinarily high percentage of times, those four magic words, "Please rephrase the question," *will work*. Why? For any number of reasons, including: (1) The questioner really was trying to pull a fast one and has now been caught. The questioner has to go back and ask a clearer or fairer question. (2) The questioner made a mistake. The words came out wrong and now he or she gets to try again. (3) The questioner is not sure what he or she has just asked, has no memory of it, and now must try something else. Whatever the reason, with this simple request, you often get a clearer and fairer question. In any event, stick to your guns. The witness has a right to clear and fair questions. Don't let the questioner ignore your polite request to rephrase.

Taking your time becomes particularly important here. To fully understand a question, the witness must apply three tests: clarity, comprehension, and comfort. Until a question has passed all three of these tests, the witness should not answer it!

Three Tests for Questions

Clarity

Clarity means only one thing—whether the wording of the question was clear *to you*. It doesn't matter whether it would have been clear to someone else. It doesn't matter whether the questioner thought it was clear, or *why* it wasn't clear. Even the best questioners phrase things badly, and even the best witnesses get distracted or confused. You know from your own experiences that even when you know what you want to say, the words sometimes don't come out right. The more you're talking and the harder you're thinking, the more often this will happen. Now imagine having to think up and ask questions for hours or days at a time. Sometimes it's a wonder that anything comes out straight. Do not be surprised or feel uncomfortable if some of the questions don't come out clearly; just don't answer them.

Sometimes a questioner won't realize, or will pretend not to realize, that a question was not clear. That's not your problem. It doesn't matter whose "fault" it was that you felt the question was unclear. All that matters is that it was not clear to you. Ask that it be rephrased, and keep asking until it's clear. If the questioner acts surprised or irritated, don't be intimidated. Keep your cool (see Rule 4) and keep demanding simple, clear questions.

Comprehension

Comprehension means that even if you heard the words, do you really understand what's being asked? That doesn't mean you think you understand why the question is being asked—just whether you understand the narrow question that came out of the examiner's mouth and will now appear in the transcript or other record. Nothing else matters at that moment.

To focus so completely on one question is hard work and it is unnatural. We're more used to a question just being part of the overall flow of the conversation: a prompt, a follow-up, a show of interest. For a witness, the actual words of the question are what matter the most. Thus, the advice earlier to treat each question as if it was the first and last one asked becomes crucial. Your only job is to comprehend what that question is asking.

As a federal prosecutor, I often spent a great deal of time preparing witnesses. The main difference from private practice was that those conversations were not privileged. If you work with your personal lawyer to prepare to be a witness, it is strictly confidential, protected by the attorney-client privilege. No one can ask you about it. However, a prosecutor's "client" is the government or the people as a whole, not any one individual witness, so defense lawyers can and do ask about conversations with the prosecutor, sometimes trying to imply that the witness has been improperly coached. Here's an example of what happens when you focus on where the questioner is going, not the question.

A good defense counsel may ask the question with sarcasm or a sneer: "Isn't it true that you met with the prosecutor?" If the witness is not prepared, you can almost see what flashes through his or her mind: "Well, yes, I met with them but I didn't do anything wrong and no one told me what to say, but he's making it look bad and maybe I shouldn't have met with them, and now the jury won't believe me if they think that happened." So from this tortured thinking, witness after witness over the years has reacted in fear and answered no to that sort of simple question. What they are trying to do is tell the truth, knowing they were not told to say anything wrong. What they have actually done is lied under oath.

What went wrong? They didn't listen to and comprehend the actual question. They were focused on where it was "going." Yet, there's nothing wrong with meeting to go over the facts. On the contrary, any trial lawyer who is doing his or her job will try to meet with witnesses before putting them on the witness stand. Listen carefully and treat each question as the first and last one, and this line of questioning goes nowhere. For example:

Q: Isn't it true that you met with the prosecutor?
A: Yes.
Q: And you met with her for a long time, didn't you?
A: Would you please rephrase the question?
Q: Well, how long did you meet with her?
A: Several hours.
Q: And during those several hours she rehearsed your testimony with you, didn't she?
A: Please rephrase the question.
Q: What's wrong with the question?

A: What do you mean by rehearsed?

Q: She told you what to say, didn't she?

A: Just that I should tell the truth.

Consider this exchange, and how easy it was to defuse the issue by just answering the questions. On the one hand, the witness is at a great disadvantage. The questioner is prepared and knows where he or she is going. For the witness to try to anticipate it is dangerous. On the other hand, many times the witness knows more about the matter than the questioner and is worried about (and anticipating) a line of questioning the questioner actually knows nothing about, or simply hasn't figured out. So don't listen to what you think the question might or ought to be asking. Take each question one at a time. Listen only to what is being asked, and then ask yourself if the question makes sense. If it doesn't, don't answer it. Just say, "Would you please rephrase the question?" If you do understand it, answer it simply, then stop and wait for the next question.

Comfort

Comfort means the words themselves seem clear, the question is comprehensible, *but* you must decide whether you are comfortable with what the question contains or the way it's being asked. The most common source of problems here comes from the *assumptions* that are contained in the question. The classic example many lawyers use is the witness who is asked the yes-or-no question, "Have you stopped beating your spouse?" It's a simple question on its face, but by asking whether you've "stopped," the question *assumes* that you "started"! You can't answer the question without essentially agreeing that you've been beating your spouse.

Almost all questions contain assumptions. Think about something as basic as "Isn't it true that it's a nice, warm Thursday today?" It's a seemingly simple question, yet it's filled with assumptions. Some are obvious; if today isn't Thursday, the problem is so apparent that even in casual conversation you might stop the flow to correct the day. Then again, if the main topic of casual conversation is the weather, or something related to it, like "What are we going to do today?" then you might not catch the irrelevant error, or you might catch it but choose not to correct it. After all, who cares? *You* know what day it is. Yet in the formal world of a witness, by not correcting it, you would have agreed with—and thus adopted as your own—a false statement.

The problem gets worse when the assumptions get more subjective. For example, in the same simple question, what does "warm" mean? If I use that word with people in Florida, it means one thing, but with people in Alaska it may mean something very different. In a casual conversation, no one is being that precise; everyone generally understands the context, and even if there is any misunderstanding, it doesn't matter that much. Here again, a witness does not have those luxuries. If you accept someone else's assumptions, you have put your word, and possibly your future, behind a statement you may not understand or agree with.

The solution is simple: If a question contains assumptions that you either don't understand or don't agree with, or just aren't comfortable with, don't answer it. Either ask that it be rephrased or directly challenge the false assumption. This is *questioning the questioner*. It enhances a witness's stature as the one in control and derails poor questions. For example:

Q: Isn't it true that it's a nice, warm Thursday today?
A: Would you please rephrase the question?
Q: Isn't it a warm Thursday?
A: I'm sorry, but I don't think it's Thursday today.
Q: Oh, well, it is a warm day today, isn't it?
A: Would you please rephrase the question?
Q: Do you know what the temperature is outside now?
A: No.

In this overly simple example, the path to comfort may seem extreme, but the discipline of insisting on it is terribly important. Remember, this is your statement, and you have a right to insist on questions you can understand, whether or not it gives the questioner what he or she wants. "What's the temperature?" is a question you can be comfortable with, whether or not you know the answer. "Nice" and "warm" in this artificially precise environment are not comfortable assumptions.

The problem arises again out of the old saying "He who writes the rules wins the game." If you adopt a questioner's assumptions even though they would not be your own, you have allowed the questioner to put words in your mouth and you have lost control of the process. The extraordinary discipline necessary to avoid this trap may make more sense when we look at common types of assumptions by questioners. Three types of assumptions are the worst—assumptions relating to *categories*, *concepts*, and *choices*.

Common Types of Assumptions by Questioners

Category Assumptions

The first type of assumption that should make you uncomfortable is when someone tries to assume categories or other types of formality that in truth do not exist. Having clear groups, policies, or lines of authority makes a questioner's job easier, both because it makes things simple and because it provides the opportunity to highlight, or attack, anything or anyone that doesn't fit in these categories. If you go along, you may be setting yourself, or someone else, up for an unnecessarily difficult time.

For example, in a recent investigation, it became important to look at how and when customers were allowed to buy a machine on "evaluation" and thus be able to return it if they wanted. The investigators were convinced that there was a group of "evaluation" transactions that were not "real" sales because the customer didn't "really" commit to buying. Yet the company had claimed them as income. Witness after witness testified that there was no distinct group of phony "evaluation" sales. Yet, time after time, the investigators tried to force witnesses to accept "category"-type assumptions by asking questions like "Who was responsible for enforcing the company's policy regarding the evaluation machines?" In fact:

1. there was no such recognizable category of deals at the company;
2. there was no such company policy; and
3. there was no one in charge of enforcing a policy that didn't exist.

How do you answer a question like this as a witness? Where do you start? The answer is, you *don't*. You ask that it be rephrased, and if that doesn't work, you ignore the question and challenge one or more of the assumptions. You don't answer whether or not you've stopped beating your spouse: You ask that the question be rephrased, and if it's not, you challenge the assumption by saying, "I've never beaten my spouse."

Concept Assumptions

Another dangerous form of assumption is when the questioner puts pieces of evidence together to form concepts—often terms or things—that don't actually exist. In the same case, a company employee had sent a fax to a vendor requesting documents about some of the machines. To get the vendor's attention and emphasize the urgency (responses had been slow in the past), someone had written the word "HOT" in big letters on the fax cover sheet. Most people would see clearly what this meant and not bother to ask questions. At most, it may have been reasonable to ask, "What does 'hot' mean?" But investigators often get so caught up in their own theories that they lose touch with reality. In this case, the investigator took this word, invented a concept, and then suspiciously asked: "What was the company's policy for dealing with 'hot machines'?" The witness was dumbfounded: he had never heard this term. It had been invented by the investigators. How should he answer the question? He should *not* answer the question; he should ask that it be rephrased or challenge the assumption: "I've never heard of 'hot machines.'"

Choice Assumptions

Another common danger is what I call the devil's choice: a question that gives a choice between two extreme assumptions. This creates two problems: First, it assumes that at least one of the assumptions is plausible, or even correct. Second, it assumes or allows for no other alternative. For example, from the same SEC case: "Did you process this paperwork immediately, or was there a practice of delaying it?" In fact, as so often happens, reality was in the middle: neither immediate nor delayed. The question was not a proper one to answer.

The other part of "comfort" is that you must be equally comfortable with your answer. The most important issue here is answering yes or no. Despite the examiner's wishes, many questions cannot be answered simply yes or no.

Listen carefully to the question, think about the assumptions it contains, and if you have any uncertainty, do not give a simple yes-or-no answer. Ask that it be rephrased, and if that doesn't work, challenge the yes-or-no assumption: "I'm sorry, but I can't answer that with just a yes or no."

There are as many reasons why you might not understand a question as there are possible questions. We have discussed only some of the more common problems. The point is that it doesn't matter why or how you don't understand. This process is too important and precise to "fudge" by answering a question you don't understand. Don't do it. Just say, "Please rephrase the question."

Wiggles and Squirms

Every parent knows that when you try to impose rules and discipline on children, they will try different ways to wiggle and squirm out from under. Questioners are much the same. If a witness imposes the discipline of insisting on clear and fair questions, of saying, "Please rephrase the question," questioners will seek to wiggle and squirm out from under and to keep doing things their way. One big difference, though, is that while children have a seemingly endless variety of wiggles and squirms, the circumstances of a witness environment leave the questioner with fewer options—basically only three. Like everything else, if a witness is prepared for these three classic wiggles and squirms, they are much easier to deal with.

1. The Court Reporter
The most common wiggle and squirm is to use the court reporter. The questioner asks a bad question, the witness says, "Please rephrase the question," and the questioner says, "Would the court reporter please read back the question." There's nothing wrong with this; on the contrary, it gives everyone a chance to take a breath and listen to it again. The problem is that, time and again, unprepared witnesses think: "Gee, if the court reporter can read it back, it must be OK." No! Court reporters are remarkably good at what they do: they do not edit, modify, or do anything to improve the

words that come out of the questioner's mouth. If the question was gibber-ish, the repeat will be gibberish.

More important, the questioner has not done what the witness asked. The questioner was not asked, "Please repeat that bad question." The request was to "please *rephrase*." Don't give up, and don't give in. If the questioner's response is to have the court reporter mirror back the same bad question, all the witness should do is to mirror back the same reply: listen, pause, then say, "Please rephrase the question."

2. The Follow-up Question

The second classic wiggle and squirm is a challenge from the questioner, in the form of a follow-up question. The questioner asks a bad question, the witness says, "Please rephrase the question," and the questioner says, "What was wrong with my question?" or "What didn't you understand about my question?" The questioner has now posed a new question, a follow-up, and we need to consider the options for responding.

There will be times when the witness can easily identify a word or phrase in the question that was troubling, and can respond simply, "I'm not sure what you meant by _____." However, the ability to be that precise, and limited, in finding a question's flaws, is surprisingly rare. Keep it simple. The truth is that most bad questions are bad, at least in part, because they are too long. When I teach lawyers how to try cases, I always warn them not to ask questions that are more than six to eight words long (which, if you try it, is very short). Longer than that, and the question is bound to be compound, confusing, and vague.

The flip side is equally true for witnesses: give the questioner the benefit of a few extra words, but if a question is more than eight to ten words long (still pretty short), alarms should go off—don't answer it. It is likely neither clear nor fair. No witness can keep track of the whole thing. It's almost certain to include assumptions, multiple questions, language issues, and more problems. So the majority of the time, the best, most truthful, and easiest response to the follow-up question is, quite simply, "It's just too long and confusing; can you break it up for me?" That's all—end of dialogue.

3. The Obstinate Child

You've seen this child—in the corner, stamping his feet in frustration, screaming, "No, no, no, I won't!" Here is the lawyer's version: the questioner asks a bad question, the witness says, "Please rephrase the question," and the questioner says, "No, that's the best I can do," or "No, I think it's straightforward." Sadly, I read transcripts all the time where unprepared witnesses obviously think, "If that's the best he can do, I guess I have to answer it!" No! If that's the best he can do, too bad!

It's the witness's testimony, not the lawyer's. Questions have to be clear and fair to the witness, not to the questioner. Why would the questioner's opinions of his own questions matter at all? Here, again, the questioner has done nothing to fix the problem with the question. Don't answer it! Just say, "I'm sorry I still don't understand; why don't you ask another question?"

The great Spanish novelist Miguel de Cervantes said, "Forewarned, forearmed; to be prepared is half the victory." The more a witness knows what's coming, the better he or she is able to deal with it. Teach the discipline *and* the response.

Chapter 19

Rule 6: If You Don't Remember, Say So

One of the most obvious rules is also the most deceptively difficult for many people: If you don't remember, say so. A witness can testify only to what he or she precisely remembers. This is not what we're used to; in our normal conversations, we rarely just say, "I don't recall," and stop. We try hard to keep the conversation moving, but the reality is that we often try *too* hard. We guess and assume to help keep the conversation going (and maybe to make ourselves look smart). *Don't do it in testimony.* If you do not have a clear and precise memory, just say, "I don't recall," and stop.

The problem arises from the essential structure of the witness environment, particularly a deposition. The purpose of a conversation is to have an interesting, easy-flowing exchange between two people. Anything one person doesn't know or remember is an obstacle to that flow, to be avoided or worked around.

A deposition, by contrast, is intended, in part, for discovery. To discover what the witness knows. To explore—and push—the boundaries of that knowledge in a question-and-answer environment requires asking questions until the witness no longer recalls or knows the answers, and then to keep going just to be sure. Memory becomes a key factor, and a key point of conflict.

Important Points About Memory

The mind is an amazing instrument, and even today experts do not fully understand (and in some areas are fiercely debating) how our memory works. However, without getting caught up in those debates, there are a few things that science, common sense, and experience tell us that are critically important here. These include:

- What's important for one is not important for all.
- The tougher the issue, the more difficult it is to remember.
- Memory fades quickly.
- Faded memory becomes random and anecdotal.
- Anecdotal memory becomes reconstructed memory.

Let's look at each of these points briefly.

What's Important for One Is Not Important for All

Most investigations, litigation, or disputes in which people are questioned are actually very narrow: They often focus on a single incident, transaction, practice, person, or entity. The problem is that what the questioner is narrowly and intently focused on may not have been particularly interesting, unusual, or significant to the witness at the time. Whether or not it now has become important for the questioner does not change the fact that it was *not* important to the witness then.

Without some special significance to you *at the time*, the chances that you will remember it now are much less. This new interest and focus are not your problem; it does not and should not change what you remember. However much the questioner might wish it, his or her focus does not change yours and should not change your memory.

The Tougher the Issue, the Tougher It Is to Remember

For better or worse (sometimes both), the flip side of the last principle is not necessarily true: Important does not always mean memorable. This is particularly so when it comes to remembering things that were either physically or psychologically difficult. The easiest examples relate to physical pain and trauma. A woman who has successfully given birth to a baby may, particularly over time, block out much of the memory of the pain of even a very difficult labor; an accident victim may block out the moments before, during, or after the crash.

The more the pain or difficulty moves into the psychological realm, to whatever extent it can be distinguished, the more complicated these issues become. The raging debate among experts over issues such as repressed memory of trauma is far beyond the reach of this book, but it is important to make note of and consider. A questioner may push you by emphasizing how dramatic or difficult or "memorable" he or she thinks a matter must have been. Whether or not the questioner is right does not mean you *must* remember the details clearly now.

Memory Fades Quickly

The pace of investigations and litigation today means that questioning often does not happen until months or even years after the events at issue. This is not your fault. You can testify only to what you precisely remember, and memory fades quickly. Your own experience tells you that after just a few weeks (sometimes less!) our memory falls off dramatically.

Try this exercise: If you know that you will be asked about a specific date or incident some distance in the past, pick another date at random around the same time, and try to remember everything you did that day. You may be surprised at how little you remember, but it should be a pleasant surprise. Your lack of memory of what you did three weeks or three transactions later should help reassure you that your lack of memory about the issue in question is real and valid.

Faded Memory Becomes Random and Anecdotal

It would make it easier for a witness if our memory loss over time was absolute—if we remembered everything back to a certain date, and nothing beyond it. That is not how memory works. As our memory fades, we forget things unevenly. We may randomly forget recent events, but remember long past ones. I may be able to tell you what I had for lunch on a particularly special Thursday way back in the first grade, but not what I had for lunch last Thursday. One is fixed in my mind, for whatever reason, while the other is not.

We may also remember, or forget, bits and pieces, leaving us with partial or anecdotal memory. Think of the classic Five Ws: who, what, when, where, and why. For any faded memory (beyond a few weeks), you have probably forgotten one or more of these component facts. You may vividly remember that family quarrel at Thanksgiving some years ago, but not which year it was. You may remember a conversation you had with your spouse while driving, but not your destination.

Why is it important to understand the random and anecdotal nature of faded memory? Because it's natural and it's important to be comfortable with it! Far too often, witnesses get into trouble because they remember only one piece of an incident or issue, but when pushed by the questioner, they try too hard to remember more. No matter what a questioner may say or imply about what you "should" or "must" remember, it is perfectly normal to remember some bits and pieces but not others. Talk about what you *do* clearly remember, and don't worry about what you *don't* remember.

Anecdotal Memory Becomes Reconstructed Memory

The real danger of not being comfortable with an imperfect and partial memory is that you will venture into the dangerous waters of reconstructed memory. Reconstructed memory is not based on what you actually recollect, but what you are pushed to infer, guess, and conclude from everything else. It is speculation—"could have, would have, should have, must have"—expressed as fact. Think about the Five Ws when questioned about a meeting:

WHO: Bob would have been there; he usually came to those staff meetings.
WHAT: We could have talked about Bob's budget only if he was there.
WHEN: The meeting must have been in November, because it was cold outside.
WHERE: A meeting that size should have been in the conference room.
WHY: There must have been a problem with Bob's budget for it to come up at the meeting.

None of us like to come across as uncertain, so too often these inferences come out as statements of facts: "Last November, Bob attended a meeting we had in the conference room to go over problems with his budget."

But suppose it turns out (or someone else testifies) that on an unseasonably cold day in September, on one of Bob's rare sick days, the staff meeting was held in the cafeteria and Bob's budget was used as a good example for others. What has happened? Inferences have been stated as facts, and the facts are wrong—or at least they have created unnecessary conflicts. Now, instead of a simple "I don't recall," the entire process has been made more difficult, and more dangerous, for all concerned.

Anything can *refresh* your memory. A document, name, description, or almost anything can help us to legitimately remember something we had previously forgotten. With a friendly examiner—your lawyer, or the lawyer for your "side"—this can be very helpful. If a friendly examiner asks you if you have exhausted your memory and you say yes, this will give him or her a clear opportunity to show you something that might help you refresh your memory.

However, nothing and no one should *re-create* your memory. If looking at documents or being asked questions does not refresh your memory of what actually happened, don't assume anything just because there is a document or a question. The difference is terribly important: in one case, you have truly remembered something; in the other, you have made something up based on speculation.

"I Don't Know" versus "I Don't Recall"

In a normal conversation, there is often very little difference between "no," "I don't know," and "I don't recall." For a witness, it can matter a great deal.

- *Details.* Every day, we see or hear so many details in our mail, conversations, work, and e-mail. Names, events, entities, projects—whatever it is, we see or hear it, and then it's gone. Don't try too hard. When asked about such details, be careful about just saying "I don't know" or "I never heard of it." The next thing you know, they may pull out a document that you saw that references it. Err, if at all, on the side of caution: "I don't recall" is the most truthful answer. Then, if the document shows up, it refreshes your memory rather than contradicts your sworn testimony.

- *Fundamentals.* On the other hand, if something is fundamental and wrong—you would never have done or said that—don't hide the truth behind memory. If you're clear that something —even long ago—never happened, say so, not "I don't recall." Deny what needs to be denied. "I don't recall" opens the door for someone else to say that it happened, however falsely, without fear of contradiction.

A witness's memory lapse creates difficulties not encountered in daily conversation. In a normal conversation, saying "I don't remember" is usually a conversation-stopper, or at least a subject-changer. The other person may try to help you remember but will fairly quickly move on to something else. Lack of memory is rarely interesting. In this artificial world of being a witness, the opposite is often the case: An "I don't recall" answer may be only the beginning of a long parade of questions on the subject. They may be aimed at refreshing your memory, pulling a fuller answer out of you, or just wearing you down. Do not give up. No matter how many different times or ways a question is asked, the answer remains the same.

The discomfort, or "memory guilt," comes in the repetition. I represented a witness in a full day of testimony before a government agency on a matter she remembered very little about. She did an excellent job of making clear what she did and did not know or remember, which meant she had to say "I don't recall" hundreds of times. During a break late in the day, she described the problem very well: "I've never been asked so many questions about so many things I know so little about." Understanding why this process was so different made it easier for her to understand why her answers had to be so repetitive.

Telling nothing but the truth often means spending as much (or more) time making clear what you do *not* remember, as telling what you do recall. That's perfectly appropriate. When "I don't recall" is the clearest and most truthful answer, you should never feel uncomfortable about giving it, as many times as is necessary.

Chapter 20

Rule 7: Don't Guess

The Danger of Guessing

Could have/could be, should have/should be, would have/would be. Ahh, guessing—we love it so. We judge ourselves, and each other, on how well we do it. Yet in the unnatural world of a witness, it is an invitation to disaster. There are three basic kinds of guessing: guessing about factual details, guessing about inferences, and guessing about hypotheticals. Consider each in turn.

1. Guessing about Factual Details

The first form of guessing involves factual details like dates, times, names, numbers, and so on. Guessing at even the most minor factual details is an easy way for a witness to get into trouble. If you are not absolutely sure, or do not know with complete precision, say so. Just say "I don't know" or "I don't want to guess" and stop. This again is unnatural but critical. In our everyday conversations, we guess, estimate, or do whatever seems reasonable to keep the conversation going, knowing that we will never be cross-examined or held to our precise statement.

The problem is that whenever you guess, there is always a chance you will guess wrong. That's usually OK in a casual setting. Everything changes when you become a witness. What we think of casually as being "wrong" really means false, and when false is under oath and on the record, or anything close to it, you have a serious problem. As a witness, you can be only as precise as you are precisely and absolutely certain.

Under Rule 6, we talked about how random and piecemeal memory can be. When we remember only part of something, we feel uncomfortable not remembering the whole thing. That discomfort can tempt you to try too hard and to guess at the missing details. Then, when the questioner looks at a document or asks someone else for the same details and they give a different answer, you have created the worst kind of conflict—an unnecessary one.

There will always be some natural conflict when two or more people are asked about the same matters; perceptions and memories will always lead to some honest differences. However, there is no reason to make things worse by guessing and possibly creating unnecessary conflicts, when you could and should just say "I don't know" or "I don't want to guess."

What happens if you give one of these responses and the questioner persists? Sometimes a questioner will want you to guess and will push you to do it. The goal may be to push you to say more, to lead to other questions, or to provide something that can then be used in questioning other witnesses. Whatever the motive, your job is the difficult one of making clear and keeping clear what you do *not* know, not just what you *do* know. In this context, this means you must

1. make it clear that you don't know;
2. make it clear that you don't want to guess; and
3. if, having made this clear, you're still pushed, give yourself (and others) plenty of extra room and make it explicit that you are guessing!

How is this done? Like everything else a witness does, one question at a time. Suppose you are being asked about a meeting that you think took place last April, but you're not sure. For whatever reason, the questioner has decided to try to use you to pin down the date. Think about how you might respond truthfully while still giving yourself a generous margin of error. For example:

Q: When did this meeting take place?
A: I don't recall.
Q: Well, it was last year, wasn't it?
A: I believe so.

Q: When last year?

A: I don't recall.

Q: Well, you were at this meeting; give us your best memory of the month.

A: I don't want to guess.

Q: What is your best guess?

A: I could only guess that it was sometime in the spring.

You have answered each question to the best of your ability, without locking yourself in to greater precision than you are truly comfortable with. It gives you and anyone else who may be asked the same question plenty of room to avoid unnecessary conflicts. Having given a range, do not let anyone narrow it unless you are absolutely certain.

2. Guessing about Inferences

The second and most common form of guessing is one we do not usually think of as guessing. Every day, every hour, in virtually every conversation we have, we draw inferences from what is around us. Not only is it common and natural, it's part of what we pride ourselves on as intelligent beings. We may call it by different names: conclusion, inference, opinion, presumption, deduction. However it may be phrased, it usually is in some way an answer to a "why?" question. Why did someone do/say/write something? What did they mean by it? Why did something happen or not happen?

If we are talking about a subject with which we are familiar, we take pride in the fact that our inferences are often correct. If we could figure the odds, we would take comfort in the chances being 90 percent, perhaps even 95 percent, that we are right. Therein lies the problem. By congratulating ourselves on the high chance that we are right, we are both recognizing that what we are really doing is guessing, and acknowledging the real possibility, however small, that we are wrong. Words like "inference" are really only fancy ways of saying "guess."

In a casual conversation, the chance that our inferences are wrong is understood and accepted by all. For a witness, under oath and on the record, it is not acceptable. It means that there is a real chance (even if it's 5 percent) that you are making a false statement, which is a serious matter in all witness situations and a potential criminal act in many. For a witness,

95 percent simply is not good enough. Either you are 100 percent sure or you are guessing. Don't do it. Just say "I don't want to guess," and stop. Remember, you can really testify only to what you clearly remember that you *saw*, *heard*, or *did*—not what's in someone else's mind. So, if you are asked, "Why did Mr. X say this?" (or "What did Mr. X mean when he said this?"), you have only two choices:

1. If Mr. X *told you* what he meant when he said that, you can testify because that is something you *heard*. Understand that you are still not saying what he was really thinking, just what he said about it (after all, he could have been lying to you).
2. If Mr. X did *not* explain himself to you, your opinion of what he meant, however good you may be at giving such opinions, is still just a guess.

Avoiding this kind of guessing can be one of the most difficult tasks facing a witness, for two principal reasons: the curse of the intelligent witness and the pressure of inference guilt.

The Curse of the Intelligent Witness

The curse is simply that the more intelligent and talkative witnesses are, the more accustomed they are to thinking that they have all the answers. Lawyers often make the worst witnesses because they are used to giving opinions on almost anything, and they almost always believe their opinions to be based on logic or reasoning. The challenge of being a witness is to discipline yourself to put these natural tendencies aside. In most witness situations, you are not there to impress anyone with how smart you are. The more you try to impress, the longer and more unpleasant your time as a witness is likely to be.

The Pressure of Inference Guilt

A questioner's efforts to use a witness's natural desire to appear smart and helpful to get more out of that witness brings out inference guilt. The tactic is to try to embarrass the witness into guessing: "Wouldn't it be logical that? . . ." "Surely it makes sense that? . . ." "Doesn't it appear from what

you've said? . . ." and "I know you don't want to guess, but you understood that? . . ." These are all ways to try to use guilt in order to push the
witness into saying things he or she isn't absolutely sure about. However,
you should never feel embarrassed or defensive about telling the truth in
a precise way. That's the job of a witness, whether or not it fits with what
the questioner wants.

3. Guessing about Hypotheticals

Look up the word "hypothetical" in a thesaurus, and the synonyms that
appear include "guessed," "assumed," and "imaginary." Lawyers are used
to hypotheticals as a teaching device: the old Socratic method involves endless succeedingly tougher hypotheticals to explore legal principles. However,
this is not an academic environment. For a witness, hypotheticals can be
a dangerous trap. More importantly, they are the worst form of guessing—using hindsight and foresight, in either the attack hypothetical or the
meteor hypothetical.

The Attack Hypothetical

The most common type of hypothetical in many cases is the attack hypothetical. This involves the questioner putting forward some assumed facts, and
then asking what the witness—or someone else—would, should, or could
have done. It is an attack hypothetical, because it is not being asked out of
curiosity. It is being asked to use the witness's answer to attack someone
else—to criticize what they did or did not do under those facts. Of course,
the witness was not there, was not involved, and was not aware of everything that the reality of the situation depended on at the time. It is guessing,
and it is often inappropriate.

The best way for the witness to think about attack hypotheticals is to
remember the Golden Rule: "Do unto others as you would have others do
unto you!" What if the situation was reversed? What if the questioner was
asking someone else a hypothetical to try to use that person to attack you?
Wouldn't you want that person to know a lot more than any questioner
can put into a hypothetical? He or she wasn't there, didn't know what
you know, didn't see what you saw, and didn't understand everything that
was involved. Wouldn't you want that person to refrain from guessing, to

avoid passing judgment in hindsight, to decline to base a critical opinion on insufficient facts? You would, so don't do these things yourself. A truthful answer would depend on far more information and inputs than even the best questioner can squeeze into a short, clear, and fair question.

The Meteor Hypothetical

With the meteor hypothetical, the questioner tries to make a point of some kind by asking a question about something that has never happened. Often, the questioner is trying to create some rule or standard by which other people, or other events, should be judged. Or the goal may be to use the hypothetical to demonstrate relationships, hierarchies, and the like. "If the CEO of the company called you and said he wanted everyone outside for jumping jacks at 7:00 a.m., what would happen?"

But if it never happened, and there is no hard-and-fast rule anticipating it, any answer to the question is pure speculation, pure guessing. In slightly more dramatic terms, it's a meteor question: "If tomorrow a meteor came crashing through the roof of your building, what are the first three things Bob Smith should do?" Who knows? It's never happened, it probably never will, there are no clear rules for it, and it would depend on the circumstances. It's the worst kind of guessing. Don't do it. Just say, "It's never happened, and I don't want to guess!"

We all want to look smart in front of others. It's natural. But in this very unnatural environment, trying too hard to look smart is a dangerous luxury. Don't do it.

Chapter 21

Rule 8: Do Not Volunteer

Question, pause, answer, stop. That is the unnatural but essential rhythm of an effective witness. We've talked about each of these first three steps; now we must talk about the stop. Don't volunteer. Like so much of being a witness, this is contrary to what we are used to—and what our goal is—in a free-flowing conversation.

The essence of conversation is connections—one thought leads to another, and the conversation flows. Depending on the setting and the people, it can meander slowly for hours or flow swiftly to a conclusion, but it always moves by means of connections. If you are chatting over lunch and your companion asks if you saw a recent movie, your response will probably not be a simple yes or no. Rather, you will go on to talk about whether you liked it, or who you saw it with, or what other movies you've seen starring the same actor or actress, or whatever interests you that's connected to the original question, or whatever follows.

Think about how a conversation like this might go:

Q: Did you see movie X with actor Smith?
A: Yes, but you know I really liked him better in movie Y. The acting was better. Of course, it may just be that the night I saw that movie was really memorable, since Mark almost got arrested on the way home. The movie went longer than we thought, so he was really speeding on the way home and saw this police car just in time. He's such a crazy driver; I'm really worried he's going to get in an accident someday.

And so on. A conversation that started with a simple question about movie X has quickly flowed along to Mark, the dangerous driver, through a series of understandable connections, from one subject to another. No one asked about Mark, or even movie Y; but in a conversation, that kind of volunteering is all right. For a witness, it is *not* all right.

In the unnatural question-and-answer world of being a witness, connections are *not* the goal. Your job as a witness is generally to answer the questions carefully, briefly, and precisely, and then go home. Question, pause, answer, stop. The questioner's job is to ask the right questions to get at the information he or she wants. It should not be the questioner's job to help answer the questions by trying to put words in your mouth. Nor should it be your job to help the questioner ask better questions or to volunteer information beyond the narrow lines of the question. You are under an obligation only to answer the question, not to tell a story. Any answer beyond the one called for is nonresponsive.

Connections mean you are volunteering. Don't do it. You may think that it will somehow help or shorten your time as a witness, but it will not. Wait for a clear and simple question, keep your answer as short, simple, and narrow as possible, and then stop. If a questioner does not follow up with more questions, and thereby misses other information, that's not your problem. Your volunteered addition may be inadmissible, irrelevant, or just off track. You have not limited the number of questions the questioner can ask, and you do not need to volunteer something that was not asked.

Think about what this same movie discussion might look like with a careful witness who does not volunteer:

Q: Did you see movie X with actor Smith?

A: Yes.

Q: Did you like it?

A: Yes.

Q: Who did you go with?

A: Mark.

Q: Did Mark like the movie?

A: I don't know.

Q: Have you seen any other movies with actor Smith?

A: Yes.

Q: Which ones?

A: Movie Y.

Q: Which movie did you like better, X or Y?

A: I'm not sure.

And so on. Each question is answered truthfully, but you have not done the questioner's job for him or her; you have not volunteered. You have *broken* the chain of connections. Question, pause, answer, stop.

There are no shortcuts here. Answer each question at its most basic level. Move forward in small, easy steps. Do not try to help the process along or anticipate where it might be going. Too often that means going off that straight and narrow path forward. Those kinds of sidesteps can take much more time in the long run and greatly add to the difficulty of being a witness. Your goal should be to give the questioner nowhere to go but forward, toward the end.

Some time ago, I represented an investment manager in testimony before the Securities and Exchange Commission (SEC). During a long day of questioning, he did an excellent job of listening carefully and keeping his answers precise and simple. It was hard work, and it went against his talkative nature. Finally, late in the afternoon, he faltered. He answered a question completely, stopped, and then thought of something related to the question that he wanted to say. Like the movie example, he answered the question about movie X, but his mind made a connection to movie Y.

The good news was that as he started to say something else, he remembered the rule, caught himself, and stopped. The bad news was that the SEC lawyer, tired of having to deal with a careful witness, picked up on his hesitation and pushed him to say what he had started to say. Before I could remind him that he had already answered the question, he was off on this tangent. Although it was actually an insignificant matter, the questioner was so intent on pursuing something that came out spontaneously that we ended up going on and on about this new topic for half an hour before it petered out and we got back to the original line of questions.

When we went out for the next break, my client looked at me sheepishly and said, "You don't have to say anything; I know what I did wrong." In an effort to help things along, he had only added to the process. His "shortcut" had wasted half an hour that would have been saved by silence.

Not volunteering means realizing that silence is OK. This is a hard adjustment. In our normal lives, silence between people in a conversation makes us uncomfortable, and we try to fill in the gaps. We all know viscerally what uncomfortable silence is. We don't like it. Experienced questioners know this. They know that silence can be a very effective tool, and they play off that natural discomfort. A questioner may use silence by simply waiting at the end of your answer, as if surely you cannot be finished, surely there is more. Don't play that game. Answer the question simply, then stop and wait for the next question. Use the silence to prepare for what is ahead, not to volunteer more of what has passed.

There are two general exceptions to "do not volunteer" that a witness and his or her lawyer might want to discuss. The first is the "simple misunderstanding" exception. If the questioner and you are not communicating and are becoming bogged down because of a clear and simple misunderstanding over a basic fact, it may be worthwhile to volunteer to correct the error.

The second exception is for core themes. Every matter has a few key themes that you as a witness may wish to get across. The more involved a witness is with the matter, particularly as a party, the more important these themes become. If witness and lawyer agree on these themes, the two of you may also want to think about whether and when you want to go beyond the simple answer to a question and volunteer information to support it.

The Witness as Artist

Some questioners may ask the witness to draw a diagram, a chart, or some other form of art. As a general matter, my understanding is that a witness cannot be compelled to create anything, so it's a judgment call. My judgment would usually be no. Your witness is neither an artist nor an architect, nor is he or she perfect. Any mistakes in a diagram, whether of people, places, perspective, and so on, where a witness might in the real world just throw away that draft and try again, become part of the permanent record. Why run that risk? If there is a simple diagram that counsel wants the witness to draw, practice it, and even then, maybe bring a good copy with you. Also, if you think the other side may ask your witness to draw, prepare the witness for that request so he or she knows it's not required and won't be badgered into it. Give the witness the option to laugh it off with stories of trying to draw for a third-grade art teacher.

Revelations

As a witness, if you are hit with a flash of insight or recollection while answering questions and it has not been previously discussed with counsel, if possible keep this to yourself until you have had an opportunity to go over it with counsel, perhaps at a break. Counsel should not be caught unprepared; and your volunteering information may cause a variety of problems.

Requests

Sometimes a questioner will surprise you by asking you to agree to supply documents or information. Do not agree to any such request on the spot; refer it to your counsel. He or she can more easily judge whether responding to such a request is appropriate or advisable. Counsel can either respond directly to the request or agree to take it under advisement and give an answer later.

Testimony is serious business. Everyone in the room has a job to do. Many of these rules are aimed at disciplining the questioner to do their job right: to make him or her ask clear and fair questions. Rule 8 is aimed at disciplining witnesses to do *their* job right. Answer the question, then stop.

Chapter 22

Rule 9: Be Careful with Documents and Prior Statements

The witness is just settling into the deposition, starting to sense that there may be a light at the end of the tunnel, when the questioner pulls out the first document. She waves it around with great flair, asks a few "isn't it true?" questions, slaps it down on the table, and even the most intelligent, articulate witness is lost, thinking, "Oh, no, she has a document. I'm in trouble now." All witnesses need preparation for dealing with documents, both to be careful with them and to *not* be afraid of them. It's not an easy task.

Issues

Three basis issues arise with any document:

- *Credibility:* Is the document accurate? But more importantly, does the witness *know* whether it's accurate?
- *Language:* Language means just that. Is the questioner quoting the document accurately—the exact words, the full sentence or paragraph, the question being answered?
- *Context:* Even if the questioner quoted the language correctly, did he

or she put it in the correct *context?* What else does the document say on this subject?

Credibility

The dictionary defines credibility as "worthiness of belief." (BLACK'S LAW DICTIONARY, Sixth Edition, 1991.) To a careful mind, that process of judging whether something is truly worthy of your belief—particularly under oath, and on the record—ought to involve a rigorous examination. Yet, we all tend to place magic into documents. "If it's written, it must be true." Even the most firmly held memories or beliefs waver in the face of mere ink on paper. It makes no sense, but it happens all the time.

The question is simple: Does the witness know whether or not the document is accurate? If not, nothing should be assumed! No document can change reality. Documents are just mechanical ways of putting what we think on paper, and they are only as accurate as the knowledge or bias or beliefs of the writer. If the writer is the witness, perhaps the witness remembers the document, and perhaps the witness remembers whether what it says is accurate. If the witness did *not* write the document, there is little that he or she can truthfully say about it.

Several years ago, I was traveling, working late in my hotel room to get ready to meet with a witness and counsel. I had the TV on in the background and heard something about a mining disaster in West Virginia, in which miners were trapped. The next morning, I was running late for my meeting, so did not listen to the radio or watch TV. However, as I left my hotel room, on my doorstep I saw a copy of *USA Today* with the dramatic headline "12 Miners Found Alive." It even had a picture of the joyous faces of the family members. Walking into my meeting, I exclaimed to all, "Wow, great news about those miners!"

Except that it wasn't true, and everyone else in the room knew it. For a brief period late that night, which happened to coincide with the deadline for *USA Today*'s hotel edition, there was a report that they were alive. Thus, the dramatic headline. But it was a false report, a mistake. By the time everyone else in the room had seen later newspaper editions or heard TV or radio news that morning, it was clear that it wasn't true. All the miners were dead.

I have kept the headline and shown it to virtually every witness I have worked with since then in any case where there may be documents. There it is, an impressive document. No one was trying to lie or deceive; on the contrary, they thought they were sharing wonderful news. And yet the headline is completely false. I show it to all witnesses in the hope that they will think of it every time they are shown a document and ask first, "Do I know whether this is credible?"

The problems of credibility relate to a wide range of documents. Some of the most common examples include the following:

The "cc" (carbon copy): A common challenge involves documents that were written by someone else but indicate in some way (for instance, cc or e-mail) that they were sent to you. You can testify only from your current memory—and it's your memory, not a cc mark on someone else's document, that controls what you can say. The cc may have been carried out, or it may not have been; it doesn't matter. If you now remember receiving the document, you can say that. Otherwise never allow someone to push you into an assumption like "I must have seen it, because I'm cc'd here." If you don't recall receiving it, just say so.

Forms: We are often confronted with forms or form language that limits how we can express ourselves. You have to choose which box to check or which line best describes your situation when really none of them do it well. Don't be defensive; you were doing your best, trying to disclose or convey information, given poor choices dictated by others.

Certification: More and more today, we have to sign documents with a certification that they are true, often under oath. And yet, more and more, we rely on others to prepare those documents. We delegate that responsibility to someone we believe is qualified to fulfill it. Every year, I review and sign my tax return, yet there are significant portions of it that I do not fully understand; I am relying on the expertise of my tax preparer. What did I do to try to "make sure" what he did was correct? I hired a good expert and gave him everything he needed; I did not duplicate everything he did after he did it.

Language

The great Yogi Berra once said, "I didn't really say everything I said." That, in essence, is what the witness must guard against:

- Are the words from a document being quoted accurately, or have they been paraphrased, edited, or distorted? Beware of questioners who want to be "helpful" by trying to "summarize" or "highlight."
- Do the words being quoted from a document, upon clear reflection now, accurately reflect reality? E-mail has created a world in which we type in haste and repent at leisure. Did you—or whoever wrote or said those words—really mean it that way? Were you—in 20-20 hindsight—accurate? If not, say so.

Context

When talking about communicating, who better to cite again than Yogi Berra: "It ain't over 'til it's over!" Has the questioner taken the words out of context? Are they explained later in the document? Is the document part of a series or chain? At a recent meeting with the government on an investigation, we were presented with copies of e-mails from salespeople in the field urging the company to engage in the same questionable practices of their competitors. Troubling stuff. But when we went back to investigate further, we found that several of the e-mails were just one step in a chain, in which the company executives adamantly responded that they could *not* engage in such conduct and would *not* "stoop to that level." Without context, the words raised suspicion. In context, they were clear and helpful. Insist on knowing—and explaining—the context.

Protocol

The goal is to level the playing field, since the questioner knows what portions of what documents he or she will use and has studied and prepared in advance. The key is to learn a process and discipline that allows you to take your time, consider the whole context, and answer precisely. A document is simply a mechanical way of putting something on paper.

Treat it mechanically. There is a very simple, absolute, three-step protocol for dealing with any document. Learn this very simple protocol, and then follow it *absolutely* with every document or statement. The simple mechanics of the process will give you comfort and free your mind to focus on the substance.

Here is the protocol to follow anytime you are asked a question for which the answer is contained in or relates to a document:

Step 1: Ask to See It

Documents are like questions: You must make sure that you understand the *whole* thing. You would never (or certainly *should* never) answer a question when you have heard only a part of it. Similarly, you should not answer questions about a document until you have read and understood all of it. Never volunteer the existence of a document. However, if you are asked a question about a document (or about something that is contained in a document), *the first step is to ask politely but relentlessly to see it.* Do not assume someone else's description is accurate, and do not guess about what it says. I am constantly amazed at how often witnesses—and their counsel—allow themselves to be drawn into a debate with a document that is not in front of them. How absurd and unfair. How can the witness possibly *win* that debate? He or she cannot. The best the witness can do is to tie, and eventually lose. Do not get drawn into such a debate. Ask to see the document!

Understand that in most forums, the questioner is not required to show the witness a document. However, if despite your clear request, the questioner chooses not to show you the document, he or she has chosen to allow you to guess—because that is the *most* you can do regarding a document that is not in front of you.

Step 2: Read It

If you *are* allowed to see a document, physically pick it up, block out everything else in your mind, and examine the document thoroughly. Read the entire document carefully, no matter how long it takes, and regardless of whether you already saw it in preparation for your testimony.

(a) It is generally none of the questioner's business what you did in preparation, and if you prepared with your own lawyer, your discussions
were privileged and confidential;

(b) Every time you read a document, you will see something new, something that you missed before, so it's always worthwhile to read it
again; and

(c) You are now reading the document with the advantage of having
heard some of the questions.

Understand that some questioners will try to discourage such a thorough
review. They are often only interested in the particular section, page, or
line that helps their position, not the full context. Thus, the questions may
go something like:

Q: Let me show you what has been marked as Exhibit 66. Do you recognize these documents?

A: Yes, I do.

Q: In fact, isn't this a set of about 25 documents relating to your company's
transaction with the ABC Company?

A: Yes, it is.

Q: Turning to the second page of the fifth document, the page stamped
with the number 386, looking at the middle of the page, what is meant
by the word "transitional"?

A: I believe that it means. . . .

Remember, this is your testimony. You are in control, and you have a right
to clear and fair questions. Picking a piece of a document out of context
is not fair, at least not until you have reviewed and considered the *entire*
document (or set of documents). Once you have done this, you may wish
to consult with your lawyer if it is appropriate, particularly if reading the
document raises or reminds you of any new issues.

Step 3: Ask for the Question Again

Once you have given the whole document careful consideration, put it
down, and ask to have the question again. Now you can focus not just

on the words the questioner may have picked out, but on the whole portion of the document related to that issue. With this careful discipline,
and by limiting your answers with precision, the same exchange might
look more like this:

Q: Didn't the company describe this as "transitional"?

A: May I see what document you're referring to?

Q: Let me show you what has been marked as Exhibit 66. Do you recognize these documents?

A: They look familiar.

Q: In fact, isn't this a set of about 25 documents relating to your company's
transaction with the ABC Company?

A: It appears to be.

Q: Turning to the second page of the fifth document, the page stamped
with the number 386, at the middle of the page, what is meant by the
word "transitional"?

A: May I see the document?

Q: OK, here it is. Now what's the answer?

A: May I read the entire exhibit?

Q: Well, if you must. [Witness reads.]

A: I'm sorry, would you give me the question again?

Q: On page 386, what does the word "transitional" mean?

A: Well, I see that I didn't write that document, and I don't want to guess
about what someone else wrote.

Q: What's your understanding of what it meant?

A: Well, eight pages earlier, at page 378, there's a letter from Mr. Jones
that explains what he meant.

Q: And what is that?

A: Well, according to the letter. . . .

This exchange is adapted from actual testimony. In the real exchange, the
questioner also asked several questions trying to get the witness to agree
to a meaning of the word that was entirely different than what was clear
from the document. Whether it was because the questioner missed the other
letter or just chose to ignore it doesn't matter. You are the witness and you

have to take responsibility for—and control over—your testimony. Be careful with documents.

Document Option Tree

What else did the witness do here that helped? He considered and followed what I call the Document Option Tree. The Tree, shown below, is a way of reminding you to treat different documents differently, depending on several factors.

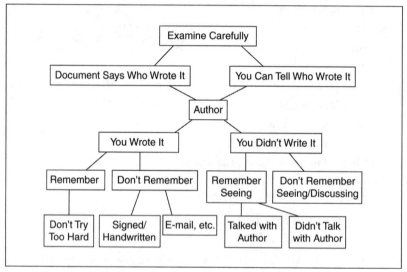

Figure
Document Option Tree

The first question is, who wrote the document? This may be clear from looking at the document (for example, from handwriting or a signature) or you may know from some other source. If you did not write the document (or don't remember who wrote it), there is very little you can say about it that's not guessing. What is it that you *saw, heard,* or *did*? If you remember reading it, you saw something. If you remember discussing it, you heard something. If you took some action as a result, you did something. Anything else (who wrote it, why it was written, what it means, and so on) is guessing. Don't do it.

Even if you did write it, what you can say may still be limited. How much, if anything, do you remember about it? A document that may be important to a questioner now may have been unimportant to you when you wrote it months or years ago, and it may be little more than a blur to you now. Just think about the numbers. Let's say that you write or in some way generate a rough average of five documents an hour during an eight-hour workday (including memos, e-mails, texts, and so on—it's probably many more!). That's 40 documents a day, five days a week, roughly 50 weeks a year. Pretty conservative numbers for many people, but they still mount up quickly. If a questioner asks you about something you wrote only a year and a half ago (in some matters, the gaps can be much longer), that means you have written about *15,000* documents since then. Put in this context, it's much easier to understand why you might not remember that one particular document clearly. That may not be what the questioner wants to hear, but it's the truth. Be careful with documents.

Two common legal concepts may be helpful here to both lawyer and nonlawyer: past recollection recorded versus present recollection refreshed. Suppose you are asked about a meeting that took place ten months ago. You vaguely remember that there was a meeting but not what was said. Then you are shown your notes of the meeting. There are two principal options, explained next.

Present Recollection Refreshed

Seeing your notes (or some other document) may refresh your memory, so that you now clearly remember all (or, most likely, part) of what was said. This is present recollection refreshed: You are answering based on what you remember now, having been reminded by seeing the document, but *not* based on the document itself. As a questioner tries to push you to answer as broadly as possible, these are important distinctions to hold on to.

Past Recollection Recorded

It is entirely possible that even seeing your notes won't help. You still may not have a clear enough memory of who said what. Say so. The best you can do then is to say that you *assume* (since you don't remember, you don't know) that your notes accurately (or somewhat accurately) recorded what you heard. They may be past recollection recorded, and they then speak for themselves. Do *not* adopt them as your memory, unless you truly remember.

Prior Statements/Testimony

People sometimes act as if prior statements have magical powers. However, a document that claims to represent a prior statement or testimony, whether yours or someone else's, should be treated just like any other document. Ask to see it, read it carefully, think about what it is, and understand what the questioner is trying to do with it, then ask for the question again. Only then can you answer a question based on it. There is no magic to this, just patience and discipline. Your job as a witness is to answer questions based on the facts, not on what someone might have said before.

If you are asked a question based in any way on a prior statement or transcript, the mechanical process is identical to that for any other document. Into that mechanical process come three important concepts regarding prior statements:

1. Insist on clarity.
2. Understand the context.
3. Remember that everyone says things differently.

You have the right to question the questioner, and the responsibility to do so carefully when someone tries to push you to agree with a prior statement. The basic process might look something like this:

Q: If X said he thought the moon was made of green cheese, would that be accurate? [Or, would you agree?]
   [Ask to see the document.]
A: May I see X's statement?
Q: No, we don't give out statements.
   [1. Insist on clarity.]
A: Were those his exact words?
Q: Substantially.
A: But not exactly?

Q: I think so.

[2. Understand the context.]

A: Did he say when he thought this, or why?

Q: I can't say.

A: It's hard to answer without knowing the context.

Q: Please answer.

[Refocus on the question.]

A: Would you please ask the question again?

Q: If X said he thought the moon was made of green cheese, would that be accurate? [Or, would you agree?]

A: I can't understand what X meant by "he thought." Was he serious, or dreaming, or what?

Take the magic out of prior statements. Remember the child's game of telephone? Everyone sits in a circle, one child starts by whispering something to the child next to him or her, who passes the secret to the next child, and so on all around the circle. When the last child says the message out loud, it's usually hilariously different from the original. Prior statements can be like that sometimes. Consider one example. Suppose that sometime before you are questioned, an investigator went out to interview a witness, and the questioner is using that witness's report:

- The witness may not have been prepared, and thus may not have been speaking precisely;
- The witness may have been guessing, and the investigator may have taken it as fact;
- The investigator may not have understood the witness's business and jargon;
- The investigator may not have been a good note taker;
- The investigator may not have turned the rough interview notes into a typed report in a timely manner (while they were still fresh), and may not have done a good job of transcribing;
- The questioner may have only read the written report, and may not have talked to the investigator about this interview to understand better what went on; and

- The questioner may not have accurately read—or understood—the investigator's report when using it to ask you a question.

The result is that you get a question that sounds as though it's based on something you or someone else said before, when in fact it is not. Even with a transcript, particularly if you are not allowed to see it, a great deal can be lost through some of these same steps. In the example above, what X really said was that *when he was a child*, he thought the moon was made of green cheese. In a game of telephone, special qualifiers like that are the first things to go.

Finally, what is the questioner trying to do? Don't let a questioner use prior statements to put words in your mouth. The most important thing is your best memory of the truth *now*. Even if, after questioning the questioner and going through the whole process, it turns out you or someone else said something different before, most of the time there's nothing wrong or unusual with that. People's memories differ and change, and people make mistakes.

Trying to use a prior inconsistent statement against a witness is called impeaching the witness. It may go something like this:

Q: You recall giving a deposition in this matter last September?
A: Yes.
Q: And you were under oath and told the truth then?
A: Yes.
Q: Do you recognize this transcript of your testimony?
A: Yes.
Q: And were you asked the following question and gave the following answer? . . .

If you were wrong before or simply remember it differently now, just say so. You should have the right to clarify any misunderstanding. If you disagree with what someone else said, just say so. It doesn't mean that anyone is lying, just that there are always differences in memory or perception. Even if you know you purposely said it wrong before, talk to your lawyer. Often there is an explanation that is important to bring out. If it's just an ordinary mistake, clarify, answer the question simply, and don't be defensive.

Chapter 23

Rule 10:
Use Your Counsel

The rules of the U.S. Senate try hard to keep the lawyers of witnesses who appear in front of Senate committees from saying anything. Yet, no matter how much time is spent in preparation, there is often still a lot a witness's lawyer can do to help while the witness is being questioned. A good lawyer will do everything appropriate to provide that assistance. So when a senator tried to keep lawyer Brendan Sullivan from talking too much during the Iran-Contra hearings, he reportedly countered, "Senator, I am not a potted plant!" He reportedly received 170 potted plants in the mail from trial lawyers around the country, and the phrase became a symbol for lawyers actively representing witnesses.

One of the reasons we break the preparation process down into these ten simple rules is that when counsel and witness use them in preparation, they can communicate better during the questioning. In almost any proceeding short of a full-blown trial, your counsel can say things directly to you or to the questioner. Good preparation with these rules can make that communication far more effective and helpful, without requiring a long discussion. Just remember two points:

1. Whoever your counsel is speaking to, he or she is really speaking to you. If a question or comment is directed to the questioner ("What do you mean by X?" "That's a long time ago.") or even to the court reporter ("Were they speaking over each other?"), it's partially for your benefit.

2. Whatever your counsel says, it's really meant to remind you of one of these rules. Therefore, don't just think of the few words your lawyer says. Think about everything you have discussed about that rule, and how it might relate to the question you have just been asked.

A witness's lawyer can help his or her client in a variety of ways at each stage of the process of being a witness. Although, as described in later chapters, there are differences depending on the type of questioning or proceeding, the types of help from your counsel may involve privilege, breaks, objections, and errata sheets, all of which are covered next..

Types of Help from Counsel

Privilege

Both lawyer and witness should be clear up front about what their relationship is. I learned this early; as a federal prosecutor, "the people" were my client, but I had no attorney-client relationship (or privilege) with any witness. If the lawyer *does* represent the witness, then both have to be vigilant to protect the privilege. Privilege issues fill volumes of case law and analysis. It can be confusing. When in doubt, stop and ask.

Because it touches on sensitive issues, it's often important to prepare the witness to discuss their preparation. Even if the substance is protected by privilege, the questioner will often ask about the logistics of the preparation: who, what, when, where, and why. That is fine, and no witness should feel defensive about having prepared for this important event. But be careful about opening the door to privileged communications. What was said remains strictly off limits, or the questioner may claim that the privilege has been waived.

Preparation with a witness's own counsel is strictly privileged and confidential. Never answer a question about or disclose your conversations with counsel. Sometimes a question that is too broad might prompt an answer that reveals something about your preparation, but do not make that mistake. For example, in recent testimony a client of mine was asked about a document that was written by someone else over two years ago. I had shown him the document during our preparation (having received it from other counsel in the case), and he could not remember having seen it before.

How should the witness respond if the questioner asks if he has "ever" seen it? The answer is that either the lawyer should intervene to set the ground rules ("I assume you're not asking about conversations with counsel"), or the witness should question the questioner to get the same result ("Would you rephrase the question?" "Would you give me a time frame?" "Do you mean other than through counsel?" or "Do you mean other than in this litigation?")

Breaks

Being a disciplined witness is surprisingly mentally exhausting. There are many things we do in our normal lives that are more exhausting in short spurts, but few that require the unrelenting intensity and focus of being a witness. What that means is that this is a marathon, not a sprint, and the witness has to prepare for it accordingly. Take breaks. Early and often. For any reason, or for no specific reason, if you need one. The challenge for witnesses is to know themselves well enough to take a break *before* they really need it, not four or five questions *after* they lose focus.

In addition to combating exhaustion and distraction, breaks can be important for other reasons. One of those is the assistance of counsel. Your lawyer is your only "friend" in the room, no matter how friendly others may seem. If the type of proceeding and local rules allow it, don't be shy about taking a break to talk to your counsel for whatever reason, and however often. Whatever a questioner might say, it does not "look bad" on the record, and it will not reflect badly on your testimony. Whether it's because you don't understand a question, aren't comfortable with a new issue, just thought of something, want to review a document, made a mistake, or just need a break, go talk to counsel (outside the room if possible).

This is your testimony: If you need a break, you should generally get one. Nor do you have to explain to the questioner why you want a break. Just say, "I need to take a short break." Also, listen to your counsel. He or she may pick up on something that indicates that you may need a break. Understand and agree in advance that if counsel asks, "Do you need to take a break?" your answer probably should be yes.

This sounds easy, but in some cases it may feel uncomfortable. After all, in a normal conversation, you don't usually get up and walk out of the room to talk to someone else, and then come back. It stops the flow, people look at you funny, and you feel self-conscious. Too bad. As a witness, you are involved in an unnatural process. Having the regular opportunity to take a break and to confer with counsel is far more important than any minor feelings of discomfort.

Know your local rules and practice regarding conferences during breaks, and prepare your witnesses for them. Tell them what will happen during a break (e.g., "I may ask you some questions if I'm confused, or you can ask me questions if you are."), or what will *not* happen (e.g., "Our local rules say that we can't talk about your testimony during breaks, so don't think I'm being rude or weird if I talk about the Red Sox.").

Legally, the general concerns include: (a) What are the local rules/law regarding attorney conferences, if any? (b) What is the local practice? Sometimes the local practice is more liberal than the actual rule, since counsel on the other side may want to confer with their witnesses at breaks too. (c) If either law or practice limit conferences, is the limit in the form of a ban, or—as in some jurisdictions—in the form of allowing opposing counsel to ask about the conferences? If the latter, that's OK. Just prepare your witnesses so they know and then conduct the conferences accordingly (e.g., "We're trying to get at the truth here, and some of these questions are confusing [or long, vague, compound, etc.], so I just wanted to ask you a few shorter questions to clarify this, or show you some of the documents the other lawyer is referring to but not showing you. Would that help you?").

Objections

If you are in a type of proceeding in which counsel makes objections, do not make the mistake of treating them as irrelevant legal technicalities. If you see a lawyer getting up to object, stop and wait. Listen closely to any objection and response and consider them carefully. You may learn something important about the question and how it could be handled from the objection.

In a deposition, the rules that govern counsel in most jurisdictions prevent objections that go to the substance of the testimony: hearsay, relevance, best evidence, and so on. The reasons for this include that a deposition is supposed to be a far-ranging discovery process, there is no judge to rule on objections, and there is no jury to hear objectionable testimony; it can be dealt with later, before the case goes to trial. The principal exception is "objection to form" (lawyers can be as lazy as any other human being, and may shorten these three words to simply "objection," or even just to "form," but the intent is the same).

The problem is that when most unprepared witnesses hear one or more of those three words, "objection to form," they assume it is some technical legal nonsense that they can and should ignore. So they plow forward, undaunted by the objection. Alas, they are only half right. There are technical legal reasons for objections to form. However, the more important half is that counsel has heard something in the form of the question—in the way it was asked—that is objectionable. "Objection to form" is shorthand for, "I have an objection to the form in which that question was asked." If counsel has that kind of a problem with a question, maybe the witness should, too! Stop, think, and unless you're certain about both what the question is and how it was asked, ask to have it rephrased.

It's important to understand that an objection is generally *not* an instruction not to answer. There are only a few areas in a deposition where counsel can give such an instruction. In the Federal Rules of Civil Procedure, for example, they are defined as follows: "Counsel may instruct a deponent not to answer only when necessary to preserve a privilege, to enforce a limitation ordered by the court or to present a motion." Fed. R. Civ. P., Rule 39(c)(2). Thus, the witness must generally answer the question, despite the objection. However, "Please rephrase the question" *is* an appropriate answer to a bad question.

In a complex contracts dispute between two health-care systems, whose cooperative effort had turned into finger-pointing, the top executive of the joint venture was called for deposition. He was an intelligent, articulate administrator who during preparation, typical of that kind of person, had a hard time understanding why he had to slow down, listen, and insist on clear questions. It took a good deal of work to persuade him, but he finally got it. In the deposition, counsel for the other side repeatedly asked questions that were too lazy, too complex, or too confusing. I would object to form, and my witness would ask to have the question rephrased.

Unable to have his way with the witness, as this lawyer (like most lawyers) was clearly accustomed to having, the questioner became more and more frustrated. Finally, he asked yet another bad question, I made yet another objection to form, my witness yet again asked to have the question rephrased, and the lawyer could no longer contain himself:

A. Please rephrase the question.
Q. You don't have to do that, you know!
(Pause.)
A. Do what, counselor?
Q. Just because your lawyer objects to form, you don't have to ask me to rephrase the question!
(Pause.)
A. I know, but it does kind of raise a red flag, doesn't it?
(Laughter.)

Exactly right. Whatever the other technical legal meanings of "objection to form," it is also a bright red flag that there are problems with the question. There is nothing automatic or universal here, and maybe counsel has not heard the question right, or misjudged it, but maybe not. Perhaps the witness should slow down, think carefully, and ask to have the question rephrased. Err, if at all, on the side of caution. "Please rephrase the question."

Errata Sheets

In a deposition or other form of testimony where the witness and counsel have the opportunity to review the transcript and submit an errata sheet, too many lawyers treat this as a trivial chore. It should, instead, be viewed as an important opportunity to continue the dialogue with your witness. Ask the witness to review the transcript with three things in mind: (a) typos and other errors; (b) things that in 20-20 hindsight the witness got wrong or simply wishes were said differently; and (c) issues or questions that have been raised by reading the transcript. Then take the time to go through all these things with them.

I am a believer in being aggressive about errata sheets—better to clarify something now than to have to deal with it down the road. There is some disagreement among jurisdictions, but the majority rule is that it is permissible to make substantive changes in an errata sheet. *See, e.g., Smaland v. Genova,* 461 Moss 214, 229 (MA, 2011). The process is not without risks: among other things, if the changes are too great, the other side may seek to reopen the testimony. However, the benefits of a clear record generally outweigh the risks.

You spent a great deal of time and effort choosing and working with your counsel before the questioning. Your counsel, in turn, has a great deal of experience dealing with this environment. Use that crucial combination of effort and experience at every stage of the process.

Chapter 24

Making an Impact

After the process of working through the Ten Rules, which can sometimes be difficult, there is often a real need to bring these important concepts together in a way that makes an impact on a witness. Over the years, we have developed one method that helps witnesses to pull together this distinction between a conversation and witness testimony and to consider in real terms the principles of "listen, listen, listen" and "don't try too hard."

The idea is to plan into the beginning of your first meeting with the witness one or more simple broad conversational questions leading to a normal conversational flow. Then, after the process of talking about the language of question-and-answer, going back to that question is a dramatic way to help the witness analyze it and show the extraordinary differences between these two means of communicating.

There are three examples of this method in appendixes C, D, and E. The first involves a witness who was a financial manager who had lived in Moscow for some time and was flown back to the United States to give a deposition in a complex financial case. The problem was that between her travel schedule, my travel schedule, and the case schedule, the deposition was coming up very quickly.

There was very little time to prepare. So the questions became: How do we pull this together? How do we drive it home? She came in and we chatted for a while. We did that introduction phase in preparing witnesses and I asked her typical questions you might ask someone: "How are things in Russia?" and "How was your flight?" Both questions naturally led to long discussions of various issues.

After a while, we began preparing her as a witness by talking about the language of question-and-answer and how different it is from a conversation. Question, pause, answer, stop. We discussed the Ten Rules. After we had done this for a while, I said to her, "Do you remember the first question I asked you?" She replied, "Well, yes, you asked me 'How are things in Russia?'" She didn't remember the other questions, so I said, "Do you remember I asked you 'How was your flight?'" She did. I said to her, "What did I mean by those questions?" There was a silence, which I ended by saying, "You can't possibly know what I meant by those questions. They are too vague." Then I handed her a piece of paper that started out with the question "How are things in Russia?" This shocked her, since none of us expect to see our conversations in print. None of us think about having our conversations picked apart.

Then we talked about the question. The first problem with that question is that its general *context* is not known. "How are things in Russia?" Since when? Compared to what? What part of Russia? It's a big country. So I handed her a page raising those issues. The second problem with that question is the nature of what is being asked. "How are things in Russia?" What am I asking about? What things? Am I asking about the weather? Am I asking about politics, the economy, the traffic, the museums? What am I asking about? I handed her a piece of paper with those categories. Third, even if you can figure out which of those general categories I'm asking about, what is the simple and most direct answer? "How's the weather? Good. How's the politics? Busy. How's the economy? Good. How's the traffic? Busy. How are the museums? Good. How's your work? Busy. How's the family? Good." That is, question, pause, answer, stop.

Really, even those categories are too broad. Pick a category: weather. What is a question that you can answer about the weather in a question-and-answer environment? "What is the temperature in Moscow today?" The question is understandable, it passes muster under the rules, and the answer is one either you know or you don't know. "I don't know; I wasn't in Moscow today. I can tell you what the temperature was in Moscow three days ago," or just "I don't know the temperature today." "When did it rain last? How hot has it been? Have you heard a forecast for this weekend?" Those are questions that are clear and simple enough to have answers. They are several levels of analysis down from the question you can't answer: "How are things in Russia?" (Please see appendix C, which spells out the steps of this exercise.)

I then went on to discuss the other question I had asked, "How was your flight?" What did I mean by that? I went through a similar series of pages. What context am I talking about? What flight? There was no nonstop from Moscow to where she was traveling. Which flight am I talking about? Even if you know which flight I'm talking about, what category am I asking about? The length of the flight, the turbulence, the book you were reading, the food, the delay, the service? What am I talking about? You don't know and as a witness, *you need to know.*

Even if you can figure out the category, a simple, direct response is all that you need to give. The length of the flight was long, the turbulence was OK, the book was long, the food was OK, the delay was long, the service was OK, and you're done. Even if you pick one of those subcategories of this question, it is better to narrow it down to specific questions that you can answer. Pick food: "Did they serve the duck? What kind of wine did they serve? Did they give out those hot towels?" Those are questions that are answerable.

Every witness needs to understand how far the distance is from "How was your flight?" to "Did they give out those hot towels?" In order to be a good witness, he or she must travel that distance and must make sure that the questioner travels that distance also. This simple exercise made a dramatic impact on this witness. She went on to do an excellent, and careful, job in her testimony. (See appendix D for the steps of this exercise.)

The same method can be used in almost any context. Recently, we were brought in at the last minute to prepare an administrator of a large health-care entity for a deposition in a complex contract case. We used the exact same method, with a slightly different question: "How are things at the hospital?" The rest of the process, as shown in appendix E, was essentially the same. The result, again, was a dramatic demonstration to the witness of how and why so much of what is appropriate in a normal conversation is, in fact, inappropriate in the precise and artificial environment of question-and-answer.

Chapter 25

Adapting to the Situation

Whatever your client's role is in a matter, he or she can be a witness under a wide range of circumstances. Some of the variables include: Where the questioning will take place? Who else will be present? How will notes be taken (if at all)? Will the procedure be taken under oath? and What will happen afterward? In addition, there are wide variations depending on who the witness is: a client versus a nonclient, a vulnerable witness, a witness for whom English is not the primary language, and more. Understanding these categories and differences can help guide your witness's responses. This chapter will address some specific circumstances. Subsequent chapters will discuss some of the most common witness environments.

The Interview Witness

An *interview* is generally informal in the sense that there is no judge or jury and it will not be recorded or transcribed. However, do not be fooled by that apparent informality. This is a very serious, and sometimes risky, process. *Every* question from the questioner, no matter how friendly, has a purpose. *Every* statement the witness makes, no matter how casual, may be written down and used. It is a difficult, often artificial and unnatural, procedure that demands your client's careful attention and preparation.

Although an interview is not "sworn" (the witness will not take an oath), it should be treated as if the witness *were* under oath. Lying in an interview like this is foolish and dangerous. It can be used against a witness in various ways; in some circumstances it could possibly mean criminal prosecution. Remind your client to think about it *as if* he or she had taken an oath to tell "the truth, the whole truth, and nothing but the truth," with the particular focus discussed earlier on "nothing but the truth."

Interviews can happen in different places: a home, an office (either the attorney's, the client's, or the questioner's), or some neutral territory. They can also be conducted by many different types of questioners: government or private investigators, government or private lawyers, and others. Moreover, they may sometimes be done with different ground rules: for attribution or not, under immunity or not, confidential or not. You need to work with your client to decide what is best in each particular case, and what the questioner must or might agree to.

Of course this assumes that you have the opportunity to speak with the witness beforehand. Get this point across to your clients: if you are ever approached to be interviewed without counsel, you should politely, firmly, and immediately refer whoever it is to your lawyer. Just take the person's name and phone number and say you will have a lawyer get in touch. This is far too important for game playing, and once a witness starts answering "just a few questions," it can be very hard to stop.

The irony here is that the testimony format, which seems much more onerous because it is so formal, actually is easier in some ways. That's because it is more obvious. All the formality and trappings of testimony—the oath, the court reporter, and so on—act as giant red flags to remind the witness constantly of the need for caution and discipline. The seemingly less formal interview setting can cause a witness to forget that discipline, lulling him or her into a more casual conversation. Don't make that mistake. Both environments require a similarly high level of preparation and precision.

The Nonprivileged Witness

There are circumstances in which counsel either is asked to prepare a witness who is not a client or is otherwise in a position where the attorney-client privilege would not apply. Many lawyers are uncomfortable preparing effectively in this situation. I am fortunate to be spoiled here; as a federal prosecutor for ten years, I prepared many witnesses of all types, none of whom were my "clients," so no privilege existed. The key is to prepare the witness on this issue as well, by taking the following measures.

(a) Talk about preparation, and how it's a common, appropriate thing, not something sleazy or suspect (e.g., "I wouldn't be doing my job, if I didn't meet with witnesses before an important trial [or deposition or hearing] like this one."), and that any effort by the other side to paint it in a bad light is silly at best (mention that they prepare their witnesses, too!).

(b) Make sure the witness understands that you are not his or her lawyer, and this is *not* privileged communication. The other side may very well ask questions about the preparation, and that's OK.

(c) Make sure you talk—early and often—about what preparation is and what it is *not*. This is *not* a "rehearsal," and the lawyer is not telling you what to say; he or she is just asking questions to find out what you know and what your reaction would be to some of the other evidence.

(d) Finally, make clear—early and often—what you *are* seeking from the witness: the truth. (e.g., "That's all I want. If I ever say anything or ask anything that makes you wonder, please stop me, and we'll fix it. I want you to be 100 percent comfortable if anyone ever asks you what I asked you to say, it's 'the truth'—no more, and no less."). Then, make sure that's how you prepare them; everything should be in the form of a question.

Obviously, there are some other adjustments to make: for example, counsel may not want to generate a transcript, or other documents or communications, from the mock deposition.

The Vulnerable Witness

In a range of cases, whether involving children, domestic violence, or other vulnerable witnesses, the witness has already gone through a great deal. How do we keep from "re-victimizing" the witness through the testimony process? There are no easy answers. There are some cases in which we wish we could do witness prep in a bubble, or avoid it entirely. But of course we can't. Here are a few thoughts.

(a) First, talk about witness preparation: explain the process, the nature and purpose of direct and cross, why the proceeding is so difficult for victims, and why it's so important that they not let the bad guys win. They're survivors: they can survive this, and come out on top. But it takes work.

(b) Second, practice giving testimony. You know what's coming. The witness needs to know, and to know how to handle it by participating in a realistic mock exam. You are not doing the vulnerable witness any favors by having an unrealistically easy preparation.

(c) Third, prepare witnesses to know they have options: slow it down, take a deep breath, have a glass of water, or take a break if needed.

(d) Fourth, be sensitive to how you can help. Are there pretrial protective orders that might limit the cross (or give you and the witness a better idea of what's coming, if you lose)? What can you do at trial in terms of objections, and so on?

The English-as-a-Second-Language Witness

For many witnesses for whom English may be a second language, there may be concerns regarding accent, vocabulary, or understanding. Each of these concerns should be addressed, and counsel must prepare witnesses to be open about the language issue. Try to take extra time—in the preparation and during testimony—to talk about their origins and their accent. Take extra time to seek out some heartwarming stories about their lives, families, and so on, so the fact finder hears them speak—accent and all—about good stuff. A key point about translators—use them. Witnesses often resist using a translator out of embarrassment, but that becomes a big mistake when they get confused or upset on the stand. Being able to manage very basic conversational English is *very* different from rapid-fire questioning. Do not make the mistake of underestimating the witness's language challenges.

Chapter 26

The Deposition Witness

Depositions are "the factual battleground where the vast majority of litigation actually takes place."

—*Hall v. Clifton Precision*, 150 F.R.D. 525, 531 (E.D. Penn. 1993)

A deposition is an important fact-finding or discovery proceeding in a civil case. Generally, any party to a civil case can conduct a deposition, although all parties can attend and ask questions. Depositions, or similar testimony situations, also happen in a wide range of government investigations, administrative hearings, and other proceedings. Although the details may differ somewhat, for these purposes we will lump all these types of proceedings together with depositions.

A deposition consists primarily of questions by lawyers and answers by the witness, under oath, with the witness's lawyer present. It is *not* a trial. No judge or jury is present, and nobody is there to keep score or award a verdict. Charm, persuasiveness, sincerity, and other appealing human attributes are largely wasted in a deposition. The principal result is usually a written record known as a transcript, which will be used (or misused) by the lawyers when the actual trial occurs. The true audience is not in the room.

Therefore, the most important task for a witness in a deposition is to keep the transcript clear and accurate. A witness very rarely wins a deposition, in the sense of convincing the questioner or other side that the witness is right. The more realistic goal is convincing the questioner that you will make a good witness by being clear, precise, and careful so that mistakes aren't made that can be used later. At the same time, the lawyer will want to work with the witness to understand what key themes, if any, both of you want to emphasize. Lawyers should review the recent line of cases attempting to restrict interruptions during the deposition.

Although it often has some of the appearances of informality—perhaps it takes place in a conference room, perhaps there is a casual atmosphere among counsel—a deposition is actually a very formal and artificial procedure. Although sometimes referred to as preliminary or discovery, lawyer and witness should treat it as a key step in the process that requires complete concentration and preparation.

To help prepare for a deposition, it's important for the witness to understand the principal purposes of the process. In most depositions, the questioner has more than one purpose, and sometimes combines all five. Each purpose emphasizes a different part of the preparation.

Purposes of a Deposition

1. Gathering Information. The questioner is trying to learn more about the matter. The witness does not need to do the questioner's job. The witness should remember Rule 5, Don't Answer a Question You Don't Understand, and Rule 8, Don't Volunteer.
2. Obtaining Admissions. The questioner is trying to lock the witness in on certain points helpful to the other side's case. Help the witness to understand what those points are—legal and factual—and to admit what he or she must, if the questions are clear and fair, but no more.
3. Testing Theories and Themes. The old saying is appropriate here: "Just because someone said it doesn't mean it's true." The questioner may raise a variety of theories, but if the witness listens carefully and doesn't agree, the witness should say so.
4. Testing and Evaluating the Witness. The witness is not being tested for his or her ability to argue with or score points on the questioner. Rather, the questioner is evaluating how the witness will appear to the finder of fact. The witness should stay focused and disciplined and be relentlessly polite. Prepare the witness to avoid getting distracted.

5. Testing and Evaluating the Opponent. The questioner is evaluating everyone in the room. Lawyer and client need to show that they are in sync: on discipline, on substance, and on responding to aggressive tactics, if necessary. The witness should listen to everyone in the room, carefully consider anything his or her counsel says, and when in doubt ask counsel.

Chapter 27

The Grand Jury Witness

The challenges of being a grand jury witness can be far more complex—and far more frightening —than those of most other witness situations. The power of the grand jury, its secrecy, the varying roles of counsel, and other factors all contribute to a dangerous environment for a witness. Worse yet, the rules and procedures surrounding the grand jury may vary significantly from one jurisdiction to another. For purposes of this chapter, we will use the federal system as the widest common denominator and the model for some state systems. However, counsel and witness *must* become familiar with local rules.

As a general matter, a grand jury is a group of citizens, chosen at random like a trial jury, but with no involvement by counsel. In the federal system, there are 23 members of a grand jury and they sit for 18 months, but the frequency can vary widely—it may be once a week, once a month, or some other time frame. No judge is present. The grand jury has two general purposes—investigation and screening—that are worth addressing briefly.

General Purposes of the Grand Jury

Investigation

The grand jury has broad powers to subpoena people and documents that may be relevant to possible violations of federal law. As federal laws have expanded over the years, so has the grand jury's jurisdiction. Once subpoenaed, a witness can be asked a wide range of questions. Although this all happens under the grand jury's authority, the prosecutor is largely in control. In the overwhelming majority of cases, the prosecutor decides who, what, and when to subpoena, the issuance of the subpoena is an easy mechanical task, agents of whatever investigative agency is working on the case serve subpoenas on the witnesses, and the prosecutor decides what questions to ask and does the asking. Grand jurors may also ask questions, but many prosecutors will have them wait until the end of the proceeding to do so.

Screening

The U.S. Constitution requires that felony criminal charges must be brought by a grand jury (unless a defendant waives that right). The grand jury must vote on whether there is "probable cause" that the defendant committed a crime in order to "return" an indictment, which is a formal charging document that begins the criminal process. In theory, it is an important protection for citizens and for prevention of prosecutorial abuse. In reality, if any screening occurs, it usually happens *outside* the grand jury: prosecutors are not required to present indictments on all cases, so if they don't think they have enough evidence, they can just drop it, or defer it.

If prosecutors do decide to go forward, though, the screening process doesn't screen out much, for a number of reasons, including:

- The prosecutor generally decides what evidence the grand jury will hear;
- The prosecutor is generally *not* required to present all the evidence, including exculpatory evidence;
- The Rules of Evidence do not apply, so hearsay is allowed, and the prosecutor can have a law enforcement agent or other witness just provide a summary;
- The prosecutor may have developed a good relationship with the grand jury, who have come to rely on the prosecutor;
- The "probable cause" standard is far lower than the trial standard of "beyond a reasonable doubt," and the prosecutor may have a good sense of how to meet it.

As a practical matter, a federal grand jury will almost always return an indictment presented to it by a prosecutor. This is the basis for former New

York Judge Saul Wachler's famous saying that a prosecutor can get a grand jury to "indict a ham sandwich." (New York Daily News, 1/31/1985, p. 3.)

Fifth Amendment

Witnesses before the grand jury have a right under the Fifth Amendment to refuse to testify if their testimony might be used to incriminate them. Obviously, this is a critical issue to discuss with counsel, but the discussion ends there: the right is broad and well-accepted, and witnesses generally do not have to explain or justify it to the grand jury. It is meant to protect the innocent, as well as the guilty. If the decision is made to exercise this right, counsel may want to alert the prosecutor in advance: in many jurisdictions, the government will not require the witness to come in to invoke the Fifth Amendment in front of the grand jury, if counsel represents that that is what will happen. If the witness does appear before the grand jury, it is often a good idea for counsel to give the witness a card to read, clearly exercising this right, to avoid any confusion or misstatements.

Immunity

The Fifth Amendment protects citizens from being compelled to give testimony that may be used against them. However, where prosecutors want to use a witness's testimony against *others*, the concept of testimonial immunity has evolved: the testimony may be compelled, but it cannot be used against the witness. The witness has been "immunized," not against any prosecution, but against his or her own testimony. This can happen in one of two ways, and it has become almost routine in some types of cases. If the witness (and counsel) agree, it can be done by letter from the government. In some cases, there are advantages to this kind of cooperation and relative informality, and it also allows for interviews outside of the grand jury. If the witness does not agree to letter immunity, then the government must apply to the court for an immunity order under 18 U.S.C. § 6003. In some cases, there are advantages to this kind of compulsion. A formal order covers only the grand jury (or other named proceeding), and not interviews or meetings outside the grand jury room.

The Room

When a witness walks into a grand jury room, there are no spectators or extras. Generally, the only people allowed in the room are:

- the 23 members of the grand jury (actually, only 16 are needed for a quorum);
- the grand jury foreperson and clerk (both members of the grand jury), who are the leaders of the grand jury;
- the court reporter (grand jury proceedings are required to be recorded); and
- the prosecutor(s).

The witness will be shown to the witness chair, sworn in, and the questioning will begin.

Counsel

In a federal grand jury, the witness's counsel is *not allowed* in the room. Counsel may wait outside, and the witness may leave the room to consult with counsel. In the words of a well-known ad campaign, just do it. This is an important legal proceeding, and the witness should not hesitate or feel embarrassed or reluctant to seek legal help if he or she is confused, concerned, or anything else. Counsel may also want to use these opportunities keep track of the Q&A, and to review the Ten Rules.

Secrecy

A grand jury proceeding is secret under Rule 6(e). That means that no one can talk about it to the witness's friends, neighbors, or employer, to the media, or to anyone else outside of a narrow legal circle. The one exception is the witness: since a primary purpose of the rule is to protect the witness's privacy, the witness can choose differently. A grand jury witness can go out on the courthouse steps and shout to the world what happened. But it's rarely a good idea, so be sure to consult with counsel first.

"Target"

Counsel and witness sometimes put emphasis on the witness's status: for example, feeling relieved that the prosecution says the witness is not a "target" of the grand jury. However, this is much ado about nothing. The government often uses three status levels in ascending order of danger: witness, subject, and target. However, the government defines "target" much more strictly than most people assume: as someone literally on the verge of being indicted. Moreover, a witness's status can change at any moment. Forget the titles; hope for the best, but prepare for the worst.

Testimony

When a witness does go in front of a grand jury to testify, it's important to remember the environment:

1. The grand jury's main purpose is to bring criminal charges;
2. Every word is being carefully transcribed and will be picked apart; and
3. Perjury before a grand jury is a specific and serious federal crime. Even a grant of immunity does not protect the witness from perjury in his or her immunized testimony.

Many witnesses have fallen for the false hope that they can bluff or bluster their way through a grand jury appearance. Prosecutors sometimes hope for this: bringing in a witness to trap them into perjury, to put more pressure on them or on others. Don't let it happen.

The Power of Knowledge

Unlike a civil deposition, where there has often been extensive discovery and exchange of allegations, documents, and information before the witness is asked the first question, the grand jury is secret. As a result, one of the most important foundations of effective preparation is trying to find out what happened, what the witness knows, what other witnesses know, and—most importantly—what the prosecutor both knows and suspects. This can sometimes be done by asking the prosecutor, asking counsel for other witnesses, researching on the Internet or elsewhere, finding alternative sources for documents, and, of course, pressing the client. The more counsel knows, the more counsel can help the witness.

Preparation

Beyond the need to discuss the specifics of the grand jury environment mentioned above, what does all this mean for preparation? It means that the Ten Rules become even more important, and even more absolute. Guessing, misunderstanding, or just trying too hard can become evidence of serious crimes. Slow the train down, whether it's comfortable or not. Take your time. Listen as you have never done before. And practicing before a mock grand jury is all the more important. All this can be done, but it must be done carefully and thoroughly.

Chapter 28

The Trial Witness

Each step along the way, including the interview, the deposition, and/or an appearance before a grand jury, is in large part leading up to a trial. Trials also take various forms: civil or criminal, before a judge or a judge and jury, or before an arbitrator, examiner, or other alternative finder of fact. For these purposes, we will call any proceeding a trial in which both sides present evidence and question witnesses in front of an independent fact finder. At a trial, the witness speaks to the fact finder, not just to a questioner.

Trials are dramatic, intense experiences, but not usually in the ways in which we have been conditioned by TV. There is very little instant gratification; witnesses rarely break down and change their story on the stand or employ other *Perry Mason*–type dramatics. Part of the widespread public confusion about trials comes from picking up sound-bite evaluations from bits and pieces of the evening news or the newspaper. The result is that we all tend to score it like a game: who did well, who looked good, or even who failed to "break." However, if testifying is a game, it is a game of slow inches, not sudden victories. Witnesses build or lose credibility slowly but surely. Because of this, it is extremely important to prepare the witness and manage his or her expectations. Going to trial is not a game of miracles; it is a game of inches. It is important that the witness understand that the judge or jury watches this whole process and puts it in the context of other evidence.

Direct Examination versus Cross-Examination

With different situations and different questioners come different types of questions. The most widely recognized and important distinction is between direct examination and cross-examination. Although this separation technically happens only in a trial or other two-sided adversarial proceeding, understanding the differences can help you in any witness situation. I have found that the best way to help witnesses understand the difference is to share how I teach these two types of examination to law students and lawyers.

In any trial or trial-like adversarial hearing, where one party or side puts someone on the witness stand, that person is referred to as "their" witness and has been "called" by that party. Which side calls a particular witness may or may not have any significance. For example, a lawyer for party A in a suit against party B could call as a witness anyone from A herself to all kinds of nonparty witnesses, to B himself. However, whenever a witness is called by party A, party A's lawyer's questioning is direct examination. Party B would then usually have the opportunity to question the witness on cross-examination. Depending on the circumstances (and sometimes on the judge), party A may then get to ask more questions on redirect, and party B may then get another chance on re-cross.

Direct Examination

The biggest difference between direct and cross-examination is usually in the use of leading questions. A leading question is one that contains or suggests its own answer. For example, "What's the weather like today?" is an open and nonleading question. You have to supply the answer. However, "Isn't it true that it's cold out today?" is a classic leading question. It contains its own answer, and is just looking for you to agree or disagree, to say yes or no.

Here are two easy ways to help identify leading questions:

1. If a question (or any part of a question, if it presents several options or parts) can be answered yes or no, it's probably leading.
2. If a question is more than four or five words long, ignoring any

introductory preamble (for example: "Directing your attention to the night of September 3, . . ."), it's probably leading.

With this in mind, the dividing line between direct and cross-examination is relatively simple. On direct examination, the questioner generally *cannot* ask leading questions. On cross-examination, the questioner can—and almost always does—ask *only* leading questions. This may sound strange or unfair, but it is actually one of those extraordinary times when the technical rules of evidence and procedure mesh very well with common sense and good trial practice. A closer look at these two types of examination may help explain why.

Direct examination comes as part of one side's effort to put on its case, to present the facts it believes to be important. The point is for the witness to tell his or her story to the fact finder (usually a judge or jury), in order for that party to understand and evaluate both the facts and the witness. With this as the goal, the questioner's job is to stay out of the way. Prohibiting leading questions helps ensure that it is the witness who is testifying, not the lawyer.

Nonleading questions should then be used as prompts and guides. Basically, at least 90 percent of most direct examinations can be covered by a simple grid, with "who, what, when, where, why," on one axis, and "else," "next," or similar words on the other axis: "Who else was there? What happened next? When was the next time you met? Where else did you go? Why did you do that?" If the question is longer or more complicated, it's probably leading, and so it does not leave the testifying to the witness. Nonleading questions also help keep the pace slower and make it easier for others to understand.

Thus, a witness on direct examination has to take a certain amount of initiative to make sure that the key facts come out in an orderly way. Other than that, all of the Ten Rules still apply. In particular, the witness should be advised that he or she still needs to listen very carefully to the questions from counsel. There is usually a point to any question; so if counsel asks a question like "Who else was there?" once, the witness should think carefully before saying "no one." If counsel asks some version of the same question again, the witness needs to think extra hard. There may be something that the witness said before that he or she is now forgetting.

It may appear to your client that direct examination is not as easy as it sounds. That's right. When I teach lawyers, I tell them that preparing for and presenting a good direct is deceptively hard and takes a great deal of work. If the situation allows for preparation, the lawyer and client need to work together intensively to make sure that they fully understand what the witness has to say, that the witness understands the order and types of questions, and that everyone has discussed the types of issues and problems that may come up.

There are some other things that the questioner can do to help on direct examination. The principal one is to help refresh your client's memory. Remind the witness to "never say never" (or "all" or any other absolute statement) unless he or she is absolutely sure. In most situations, the better advice is that of Rule 6, If you don't remember, say so. Often, once the witness says that his or her memory has been exhausted, the questioner may be able to use something to help refresh it. The most common thing to use is a document or prior statement, but anything can do it. Lawyers sometimes say that you can refresh a witness with a ham sandwich (as in: Q: "I show you this object. Does it refresh your memory about what the defendant said?" A: "Yes, now I remember that he called the officer a pig!"). All right, as long as it truly refreshes memory.

Cross-Examination

On cross-examination, everything changes. The witness has already told his or her story on direct. The point of cross is not to allow the witness to repeat or elaborate. Rather, it is usually to pick and choose certain things to either highlight or attack, or to challenge the witness's credibility. The questioner takes center stage to make points and try to control the witness. The principal tool to do this is the leading question. In fact, most of the time on cross, a questioner should ask *only* leading questions and try to limit the witness to saying only yes or no in response.

Thus, cross-examination can be the most adversarial witness situation. Dealing with it as a witness requires a high level of listening and precision. All of the Ten Rules apply, but the following are worth highlighting briefly in this context:

Rule 1: Take Your Time

Responding to these types of questions takes great care. A questioner who is well prepared will try to set up a rapid-fire pace that does not allow that kind of calm reflection. Remind your client that it is his or her testimony, and to slow it down.

Rule 2: Always Remember You Are Making a Record

This is *your client's* testimony; don't allow a questioner to put words in his or her mouth. A leading introductory phrase like "Isn't it true that . . ." or "Didn't you testify that . . ." may *not* always be true, or at least may not be phrased in a way the witness would be comfortable with. A witness doesn't have to adopt the questioner's words as his or her own. "Is it fair to say? . . ." probably *isn't*.

Rule 4: Be Relentlessly Polite

In this environment, performing before judge, jury, client, or anyone else, some lawyers are likely to come on aggressively. This is not some macho game. The witness must match the questioner's aggression with calm and focused energy on the substance, not on the fireworks.

Rule 5: Don't Answer a Question You Don't Understand!

As hard as a questioner may try in phrasing them, many questions simply cannot be answered with a yes or a no. Remind the client to be patient and unflappably stubborn in refusing to give such an answer when it is not appropriate. Also, the client must be careful of long or compound questions. If a question has several parts, you can be sure there will be disagreement about which part the witness answered if he or she doesn't make it clear. The witness should ask to have the question rephrased, or at least broken down into its various parts.

Rule 7: Don't Guess

Using leading questions, a questioner will try to push the envelope of a witness's knowledge. Tell your client not to go along with it. The witness should not go beyond what he or she clearly and precisely knows and remembers.

Rule 9: Be Careful with Documents and Prior Statements

Trying to use prior statements to impeach or contradict a witness is classic cross-examination technique. Advise your client not to get flustered, and to remember the careful process you discussed.

Rule 10: Use Your Counsel

If there are objections during cross-examination, this is not a time to relax and take a break. Rather, the witness can learn a lot about what is really going on from the lawyers' exchanges and the judge's comments. Your client should be reminded to take full advantage of that opportunity.

Chapter 29

The Party Witness

The Ten Rules apply most directly to the classic neutral witness—someone who is not a directly interested party and who has no real stake in the matter. In that situation, the ultimate goal is simply to go home, with as little risk or complication as possible. In order to achieve this, the witness must listen carefully, answer truthfully, closely define his or her little piece of the larger jigsaw puzzle, and let others worry about the big picture. Question, pause, answer, stop. Doing this well requires preparation and discipline, but that is what the Ten Rules are for.

What happens when the witness *is* an interested party—or is someone who, depending on the quality of the encounter, could turn into one? This can take many forms: the complainant or target in an investigation or inquiry, the plaintiff or defendant or director or officer of a party entity in civil or criminal litigation, or a party in any other form of proceeding. In this situation, the witness *does* have an interest in seeing, and in shaping, the bigger picture. There is more at stake, and persuasion becomes a far more important part of the mission.

Perhaps surprisingly, the changes created by being a party should not be that dramatic. Remember, the point of these Ten Rules is to help your client tell the truth in this unnatural and precise environment. They take away a lot of spontaneity, but what they ultimately give back is credibility. They help you teach your client to give testimony that is nothing but the truth. The process may be frustrating and difficult, but the result works. Witnesses who have a clear interest in the matter often lose credibility because they try too hard to persuade, to make the facts more favorable, and to make themselves look good.

What is needed is a careful balance of these competing forces; where and how to strike that balance will vary from one case to another. Finding the right balance can be accomplished only by working closely with your client. However, it may be helpful to mention some of the issues that are a part of this process.

Helping Your Client Find the Right Balance

Understanding

Where you stand depends on where you sit. What may be obvious to your client based on his or her knowledge of and position in the matter is probably *not* obvious to others. If it is to become obvious to them, it will happen because the witness has led them to that view with facts and gentle persuasion, not pushed them there with strident opinions and anguished pleas. The Ten Rules are intended to help you train your client to give the facts simply, without preaching. This becomes *more* important for a party—not less—because others may assume that the witness is biased and may become even less interested in the opinions he or she gives. An interested-party witness doesn't have to hide his or her strong feelings on the matter, but those feelings cannot interfere with the clarity and precision of answers to questions posed on the witness stand or at a deposition.

Personality

A nonparty witness's personality doesn't really matter. Certainly, such a witness is not there to offend anyone; however, as a nonparty witness, your client also doesn't need to worry about how much others like him or her. That's not the point. As a party, your client does have to work a little harder to be personable and persuasive. As counsel to a party witness, it's important for you to help your client get the right balance without trying too hard.

Emotions

The witness should try to avoid emotions in most situations; advise the witness to stay cool. If your client is an interested party, no one wants or expects an emotionless robot to appear on the stand. However, emotions can quickly overcome your client's ability to listen, think, and respond carefully. Good advice is to slow down. Take all the time needed. Make clear how you feel if it's appropriate, but don't let your feelings make you less clear.

Core Themes

Lawyers' conventional wisdom about depositions, and, indeed, some other forms of testimony, has always been to disclose as little as possible—for the witness to say as little as needed, then get out. There is still some wisdom in this. After all, a deposition is generally called by the other side, for them to ask questions to try to build their case. Naturally, it would seem, the less the witness gives them, the less they gain for their case. Keep your mouth shut, the thinking goes, and you can live to fight another day.

However, as a fundamental guiding principle, that conventional wisdom is often outdated and wrong. Litigation today involves increasingly prolonged and extensive discovery, motions, and other pretrial stages. Judges may get more involved at earlier stages, and there is increasing cynicism all around. With these and other changes, it has become more and more important for *all* sides in litigation to start as early as possible to take and hold the high ground: to get their story, their facts, and their perspective across early and often. Thus, every communication in litigation—whether a letter or a deposition—is an opportunity to tell your story. These opportunities should not be squandered.

Yet communicating your story through testimony must be done in the same way we approach every other part of the witness experience: with careful preparation and discipline. Many years ago, I heard an attorney tell a witness he was preparing: "If they pitch a slow one over the plate, hit it out of the park!" I confess, I cannot do this in softball, and I certainly don't know how it helps a witness to try it. The better game analogy, if there must be one, is the child's game of tag. In my memory, there was always something—a tree, a lamppost, a fire hydrant—that was home base, and you were always safe at home.

The key here is for witness and counsel, working together, to put together a few basic core themes for the case that become the witness's home bases. The witness can be comfortable with them, and come back to them as often as they are helpful; the witness is always safe at home. The core themes should be three to six short, simple statements that allow Juror #6 to truly understand and appreciate your case. Once you have agreed on your core themes (though agree with flexibility; they often change as you move forward with the case and learn more), they should help frame all depositions, discovery, motion practice, and trial. Your testimony should support them, your experts should explain them, and your arguments—to the judge and later to the jury—should present them.

For witness preparation purposes, the question is: What are the most important concepts that must be communicated through your client? Find them and keep coming back to them.

Chapter 30

The Expert Witness

In an age where knowledge has become increasingly specialized, the importance of experts in the courtroom has increased significantly. Expert witnesses often play a vital role as witnesses in cases requiring the scientific evaluation and interpretation of facts that are beyond the capabilities of laypersons. Expert witnesses can also serve to advise the lawyer in the investigation of technical cases and guide the lawyer through the discovery process.

Expert testimony, in federal court, is based upon Rule 26 of the Federal Rules of Civil Procedure, which among other things, provides for disclosure of experts (Rule 26(a)(2)(A)), providing a written report (Rule 26(a)(2)(B)), and depositions of experts (Rule 26(b)(4)(B)). However, at a more basic level, counsel's role is really based on an old slogan for the Syms clothing store, "An educated consumer is our best customer." We as lawyers have to be educated consumers of this type of information.

Three General Rules

While experts have proven to be invaluable in the courtroom, many lawyers underestimate the amount of preparation required to maximize their contributions. The Microsoft antitrust case illustrated some of the basic pitfalls that could have been avoided if both the lawyers and witnesses had been adequately prepared. In that case, high-priced experts floundered and were skewered with their own words, and a critical videotaped computer demonstration turned into an embarrassing disaster. The result of the Microsoft case was that highly touted lawyers found themselves in trouble in the courtroom. They may have violated three of the most basic rules for dealing with experts, discussed next.

1. "Just Do It"

It's too easy with expert witnesses to let the preparation sessions slide. And it's too easy to assume that experts know at least as much about being a witness as they know about their area of expertise. However, the reality is that many lawyers do not adequately prepare witnesses. This means that many professional witnesses who have testified numerous times may have just developed bad habits about being a witness that are now deeply engrained and limit their effectiveness. The number of times someone has been a witness should not give you any unreasonable degree of comfort and certainly should not replace the need for you, as the lawyer, to insist on proper preparation.

"Just do it" is often easier said than done. Convincing the expert who is reluctant to prepare—whether because of misunderstanding, ego, time, or whatever—takes perseverance. Here are a few different approaches:

Specialization: It's not uncommon for experts to say, "I've testified umpteen times before, so I don't need to prepare again." However, when you probe that, you may find out that although the expert's court appearances have not been exaggerated, if you narrow it to your particular case and the expertise that you need, the expert probably has not testified much—if at all.

Collaboration: Bring the expert onto your team so that it's more of a collaboration—what the expert can do to help you and to help the client. You're all in it together. Dealing with someone who has an ego, you have to appeal to that and ask the expert to teach you about what he or she knows. Talk about your need to learn from the expert so that you can do a good job.

Command: You should have as much or more of a command of the facts as the expert does, so you can gently work in your theory of the case to help facilitate his or her understanding.

Commitment: You have to demonstrate your commitment to the case and use that to flatter the expert, to allow him or her to help you with this commitment. This is our case. We have a responsibility to our client to make this happen.

Knowledge: What else do you know about this case that the expert doesn't know? You may know the lawyers involved, the parties involved, or the judge involved, any of which may be helpful to the expert.

Distinction: This is an unusual case. We know the substance. We're not just talking in generalities and we're not just saying we want to prepare you because we always prepare witnesses. We want to show our commitment to the case, the issues, and to the need for preparation as a result.

2. Know the Territory

A trial lawyer must know everything possible about every piece of evidence and every witness. You cannot allow the expert witness to be your only source of information. You have to become fluent on the issue, the relevant law, and the witness. It takes time and energy to do this work yourself. There are no shortcuts. Before hiring the expert witness, you must become an expert, both in the field in question and in the specific area of the law. This will allow you to have a greater understanding of the type of questions you must ask during an interview and the type of expert you need to hire for the case. Moreover, you should hire the expert early in the litigation process. This expert will guide your discovery and lead you through inquiries that you may have never considered.

Expert witnesses should be prepared to deal with any documents that may be introduced at trial. In a civil case, both sides usually have each other's documents. Witnesses are rarely confronted with new documents, so they can and must be carefully prepared to handle whatever is out there. While this is a basic tenet in trial practice, in the Microsoft case, witness after witness from Bill Gates on down was repeatedly tripped up and roughed up by prior statements, memos, and e-mails. There is no excuse for failing to prepare witnesses for such predictable attacks. No amount of preparation can hide problem documents, but it can certainly help witnesses deal with them effectively, and to do less harm to their credibility and to the case.

Knowing the territory means that you must become an expert in the substantive field. You must be able to understand what the expert is telling you, what you need to tell the jury, and *how* you need to help the expert communicate. Additionally, you must also be familiar with the expert witness because most experts have usually testified in the past. This past testimony will allow you to predict how well the expert will do as a witness and what the expert will have to say. Following this basic rule would have been beneficial in the Microsoft case, where the credibility of Microsoft's lead expert was badly damaged when his testimony differed from articles he had written and testimony he had given in two other cases for Microsoft. At one point on the stand, according to news accounts, he became so flustered that he mused aloud, "What could I have been thinking?"

3. The Lawyer Is the Captain of the Ship

When things go wrong in the courtroom, it's easy for lawyers to blame the client, the witness, or someone else, but it's wrong. In a trial, the lawyer is in charge. Only he or she knows the case and the rough seas through which it must sail. We cannot afford the luxury of ceding control of our case to the expert. As the lawyer, you are responsible for what that expert has to say and what that expert does. You are responsible for his or her mistakes, and you are responsible for the structure of his or her testimony and the structure of the case.

In the Microsoft case, the worst example of what went wrong went to the heart of what Microsoft and its lawyers should have done best. To counter an important piece of government evidence—software that could separate Microsoft's Internet browser from the Windows program—a Microsoft witness offered videotape of a computer demonstration. Microsoft's lawyers should have been intimately involved in the production of this video, making sure that it was clear, accurate, and unshakable at each step along the way. As it turned out, if the lawyers were involved, they were asleep at the wheel. Computer students working with the government could plainly see that the wrong software had been used. Counsel for the Department of Justice was able to confront the witness with devastating impact. In the end, he was able to dramatically ask the witness whether the truth mattered to him, and the evidence seemed to indicate that it did not.

On a more positive note, the lawyer should also take responsibility for how key concepts are introduced to a jury. Expertise is wonderful, but part of the lawyer's job is to understand that the first goal of an expert's presentation is to bring the jury up to a level where they can follow what the expert is saying. This can involve insisting on basic demonstrations and other forms of testimony on things some experts might think are too basic but are in fact essential foundations for more complex testimony.

Checklist of Issues

There are a series of key issues for expert witnesses, including the following.

Qualifications. Start early on this, because Rule 26 of the Federal Rules of Civil Procedure requires that the parties disclose qualifications quite early in the process. Think broadly about qualifications. We tend to look at the expert's curriculum vitae and just take the qualifications at face value. Sometimes that is adequate, but sometimes it's not. Formal or informal education, formal or informal training, work experience, family experience, teaching experience, military experience, and much more, can add color and depth to the basic curriculum vitae.

Understand that part of qualifying the witness is also humanizing the witness. Being a witness generally is a dehumanizing process. Question, answer, question, answer. Being an expert witness is an even more dehumanizing process. Counsel has to help experts to overcome that, and to help witnesses to humanize themselves, and to humanize their professional life, as we deal with qualifications, because qualifications can be such a dry topic otherwise.

Compensation. Rule 26 requires counsel to reveal the witness's compensation, and we have to get the witness comfortable with that. Make sure the witness understands that he or she must be open and clear about it. He or she must become comfortable with it and understand that it is common. That takes practice for many experts.

Assignment. Whether it's in the expert's retention letter or in another document, there should be a clear understanding of the nature of the assignment. It should be a short, clear statement, perhaps bringing in the elements or the jury instructions to link that to your assignment. The goal is for the expert to have an easy explanation of what he or she has been assigned to do, and an understanding of the relevance when it's tested: "I know I didn't do that. That was not the assignment that I agreed to." The assignment may change as the case goes along, but it's an important place to start.

Prior writings and testimony. Rule 26 requires a list of publications authored in the previous ten years. That's a lot for some witnesses. Make sure that the expert has searched for and read his or her prior writings on point recently and that counsel has done so as well. It is counsel's obligation on behalf of the client to use the Internet, to use other resources, and to use the library, in order to make sure to have everything that might touch on this issue.

Bias. Bias comes from a number of different sources, including that the expert witness:

- testifies only for one side or the other.
- derives a lot of his or her income from one lawyer or one law firm.
- derives a lot of his or her income from one defendant, from one entity, or from one industry.
- testifies for a particular cause.

The indicia of bias can include how often—and in what number or percentage of cases—the expert is retained for one side or another, or one party or another, and what percentage of the expert's fees relate to that one particular source. It's too late by the time you've selected your expert for you to change history. But counsel needs to know the history and prepare the witness to find the best ways to be up-front about it

Materials Consulted. Rule 26 requires disclosure of materials the expert consulted. Push to determine what materials the expert consulted that are both supportive and problematic. One of the best things you can obtain from your expert witness is insight on what is out there that may be used against your case. Make sure that the expert witness understands not to be led too easily into branding something as authoritative or as some other magic word that has legal significance.

Testimony

The Audience Gap is a common problem with experts. The expert loses track of who the real audience is. Experts spend their lives talking with other experts. That's who they work with. How are they going to share that knowledge with the real audience? Give your expert witnesses an audience they can understand. They are teaching. Help them understand who they're teaching. Almost every fifth- or sixth-grade class has a parents night or a professions day. Ask the expert to imagine being called in to a nephew's fifth- or sixth-grade class for professions day. Ask the expert to remember that context and see how it would work.

Daubert

The seminal case of *Daubert v. Merrel Dow Pharmaceuticals,* 509 US 579 (1993) sets out requirements for expert witnesses. But we should not view the *Daubert* requirements as hurdles. We should view them as page headings for our witness outline. If you use these as part of the guide for preparing a witness and having a witness testify, you do three things. One, you make sure you've covered the bases. Two, you bring out far more information than you anticipated. Third, you help put the judge at ease, because he or she hears the language that is familiar.

The *Daubert* factors are often referred to as, "Helping Counsel to Open the Gates." They are:

1. Based on sufficient facts or data;
2. Reasoning testable/tested;
3. Publication/peer review;
4. Error rate;
5. Generally acceptable;
6. Applied reliably to the case.

Anticipating Cross-Examination

Anticipating cross-examination requires three steps with every witness. First, probe what the issues are for that witness. Second, ask what the witness anticipates for cross-examination. If you were the opposing counsel, what would you ask? What will the expert say that may differ from what the witness has to say? And what is the witness most concerned about in his or her testimony? It's critical to use the expert to help understand what's coming, so you can then help the expert prepare to deal with it. Third, practice. I believe very strongly in the benefits of doing a dry run with every kind of witness, both lay witnesses and expert witnesses.

Explore with experts the potential traps for them in the hypothetical questions they're going to get. First, of course, is the incomplete hypothetical, a hypothetical that omits key facts. Most hypotheticals lawyers ask are woefully incomplete. The witness has to be listening for what's missing, and be prepared to say, "I can't answer that because it's not complete," or "It would depend on other things."

A second trap is the hypothetical that assumes facts that are not in evidence or that are not true. Help the witness to listen to the entire question, then be prepared to say, "I haven't seen anything like that," or "I've reviewed the evidence and that's not in the evidence that I know of."

Third is a trap of pure speculation, what I call the meteor question, explained in chapter 20 under the discussion of guessing about hypotheticals. To reiterate, the meteor question is a question that's based on something that's never happened and that is pure speculation. "If tomorrow, a meteor crashed through the roof of the building, what are the first three things that the chief executive should do?" It's an absurd question. It's never happened, it likely never will, and we have no policies or standards for it..

The challenge for an expert witness is understanding when a yes-or-no answer is appropriate, whether it's to a hypothetical question or to other questions. No expert is going to gain by being completely obstreperous. That's not what we want. But every expert needs to understand that it's not nearly as easy to speak in yes-or-no answers as a lawyer may want it to be. Here is a wonderful saying from the Greek mathematician Pythagoras: "The oldest and shortest words, yes and no, are those which require the most thought." As quoted in *Numerology for Relationships: A Guide to Birth Numbers* (2006) by Vera Kaikobad, p. 78. Use it with experts and help them to understand.

Those are the basic issues to think about in preparing your expert witness. A quote from *Daubert* is instructive: "The balance that is struck by the rules of evidence is designed not for the exhaustive search for cosmic understanding, but for the particularized resolution of legal disputes." To put it more simply, from the case of *Kerstetter v. Commonwealth,* 404 Pa. 168, 173 (1961), "Expert opinion is only an ordinary guess in evening clothes." It is, of course, our job to design the clothes.

Chapter 31

The Corporate Representative Witness

A corporate representative witness is a fiction for a fiction: a fictional (legal) entity providing a fictional (legal) representative. However, the corporate representative witness is an increasingly common part of many kinds of litigation and other proceedings. Rule 30(b)(6) of the Federal Rules of Civil Procedure, which governs such witnesses, has become so commonplace that lawyers often use just the rule number to describe a "30(b)(6) witness." Most states have similar rules, often remodeled after the federal one, so for clarity, we will use the federal rule here. The rule's purpose is clearly stated in the Notes:

> The new procedure should be viewed as an added facility for discovery. . . . It will curb the "bandying" by which officers or managing agents of a corporation are deposed in turn but each disclaims knowledge of facts that are clearly known to persons in the organization and thereby to it.
> FED. R. CIV. P. 30, Advisory Committee's Notes (1970).

Issues Pertaining to a Corporate Representative Witness

Working with a corporate representative witness involves covering five basic issues: entity, notice, witness, knowledge, and preparation. Each will be briefly addressed next.

Entity

In its notice or subpoena, a party may name as the deponent a public or private corporation, a partnership, an association, a governmental agency or other entity.
FED. R. CIV. P. 30(b)(6).

There are several entity issues to consider in responding to and preparing for a corporate representative deposition. First, has the correct entity been named correctly? Is it clear which entity has been named? In many situations there may be multiple entities with similar names.

Second, is the best witness actually within that entity? Complex, multitiered, or multiheaded corporate structures are increasingly common. The best—or at least the most knowledgeable—witness may actually work for a different entity. That's OK—the subpoenaed entity can select someone who is not an employee—but consider what additional lines of questioning that may open up.

Third, how broad is the definition? It is not limited to corporations or other traditional business structures. Indeed, as the Rule's Advisory Committee Notes explain:

[T]he deposition process can be used to reach information known or reasonably available to an organization *no matter what abstract fictive concept is used to describe the organization.*
FED. R. CIV. P. 30, Advisory Committee's Note (2007).

Notice

In its notice or subpoena, a party . . . must describe with reasonable particularity the matters for examination.
FED R. CIV. P. 30(b)(6)

The process of defending the deposition starts with setting this bar fairly high. For example, "the requesting party must take care to designate, with painstaking specificity, the particular subject areas that are intended to be questioned." *Prokosch v. Catalina Lighting*, 193 F.R.D. 633, 638 (D. Minn. 2003). Counsel should oppose language such as:

- "any matter relevant to the case"
- "including but not limited to"
- "any and all" regardless of time or geographic scope.

Begin the process of narrowing the notice as soon as possible. First, by negotiation and agreement with the other side (be sure to follow up any oral discussions with written confirmation—by e-mail or letter—to create a record showing your attempts, and reasonableness). If those efforts are not successful, seek a protective order or other relief, including:

- Notice is not "reasonably particular."
- Notice is overbroad—topics are irrelevant.
- Organization does not/cannot have knowledge on topics.
- Trade secrets and/or confidential information are involved.
- Privilege is asserted.

Witness

In most jurisdictions, the entity has broad discretion in choosing its corporate representative witness. Some deposition notices still ask for the "person most knowledgeable" on the topics. But that's not what the rule requires. As long as the witness has been adequately prepared to bind the corporation with his or her answers, it doesn't matter whether others in the company know more about the topic. *PPM Fin., Inc. v. Norandal USA, Inc.*, 392 F.3d 889, 894–95 (7th Cir. 2004). While preexisting knowledge may be helpful, it should be balanced against other factors, such as intelligence, other issues that may be voiced through a particular witness, experience and ability as a witness, and more. The entity may even designate a former employee if no current employee has knowledge.

Knowledge

The entity has a "duty to educate" its designee so that he or she can testify fully on the entity's knowledge on the areas in the notice. That education should include review of relevant documents and depositions, talking with past or present employees, and other available sources. Failure to adequately educate the witness can result in delays, additional depositions, and sanctions. In many cases, courts have held that a corporate designee who professes a lack of knowledge on a topic listed in the subpoena is the equivalent of a witness failing to appear at all.

Preparation

With an ordinary fact witness, preparation often involves a strategic question of how much it is desirable to educate the witness. In some situations, it may be easiest and most appropriate for the witness to truthfully say "I don't know," or "I don't recall." For a corporate representative witness, there is no such choice: education is a critical part of preparation. The first step is to help the witness understand this artificial and unnatural role. The witness is no longer Jane Smith, she is the entity: she speaks for and as the entity. That may be an easy legal fiction for lawyers to grasp but for most laypeople it is not.

After that, it's all about the notice. Review each item carefully with the witness: Does the witness understand it? What does the witness understand it to mean? How much does the witness know about it? Where would the witness look to learn more? Who would be able to help?

Work with the witness and the client to create an exhaustive list of materials for each topic: documents, depositions, correspondence, and so on. The witness must review these, even if they are voluminous. Be careful, though, about exposing privileged or other sensitive documents. Consider what documents, if any, the witness should bring to the deposition, and how to use them (e.g., "I want to be precise about that, so let me just double-check the document.")

Prepare for questions beyond the topics listed. Explain to the witness that refusing to answer, or instructing the witness not to answer, are extreme measures to be reserved for only the most important issues. If the question or subject matter is not too outrageous, or harmful to the entity, it may be worth answering. If necessary, counsel may interpose an objection, making clear that the question is beyond the scope of the notice, and that the witness, therefore, is not speaking for the organization.

Anticipate and prepare for common corporate representation questions, such as:

- Why you? (Object, but there may be related questions.)
- Who else would know?
- Who would know more?
- How did you prepare?
- What did you review?

A key question for these witnesses is whether to provide or create materials to assist their testimony—and their memory. Rule 30(b)(6) of the Federal Rules of Civil Procedure states that notices can include a long laundry list of topics, and it is often unrealistic—and even dangerous—to expect the witness to be at his or her best responding to all of them simply from memory. Consider working with the witness to develop an outline, or other materials, of at least the key points and facts for each topic on the notice. Representing an entity is a difficult challenge. Taking the time and effort to prepare correctly can make an enormous difference.

Chapter 32

The Physician as Witness

Physicians are in many respects highly intelligent, well-educated, caring, and articulate. However, doctors often fail to succeed as witnesses. Why? More often than not, we as lawyers fail them in the critical process of preparation. Preparing the physician witness poses significant challenges. As in medicine, the difficulties vary from one "patient" to another. Nevertheless, we need to work much harder to diagnose the disease, understand the symptoms, and apply successful treatments.

The process of being a witness is very difficult and unusual for anyone. It is especially difficult for well-educated professionals and particularly for doctors. Doctors, like many other professionals, have the curse of the intelligent witness. They are too accustomed to using their words and talking their way out of situations, and as a result they make the worst types of witnesses.

The first and most important thing to say about preparing the physician witness is, once again, "just do it!" There are a million excuses for not spending adequate time in preparation: your schedule, the doctor's schedule, your discomfort, the doctor's discomfort. None of them matter. Only counsel can fully understand the risks to an unprepared witness and what real preparation requires, so it is counsel's obligation to push hard to make it happen. You are not properly representing your client if you allow a witness to appear without thorough preparation. Finding the time to work together can be the first tough but essential challenge.

Key Challenges Doctors Face as Witnesses

The practice of medicine and trial practice are polar opposites. Doctors engage in prospective problem solving, working together in an atmosphere of mutual respect, attempting to determine the best treatment for a patient, and then implementing the treatment based upon that joint problem solving. As trial lawyers, we often engage in retrospective blame. Doctors are not accustomed to an environment in which they don't have that respect, don't have that joint effort, and getting the best result is not necessarily the goal.

Roughly speaking, four key concepts help explain why physicians so often have problems as witnesses. These Four Es help explain the challenges doctors face as witnesses and the challenges lawyers face in preparing them: environment, expertise, ego, and emotion. While all four are intertwined, I will briefly address them separately next.

1. Environment

Doctors are accustomed to a collegial, problem-solving environment in which they are respected, in control, and wholly dedicated to the patient's best interest. As we all know, that is not what litigation is all about. Long before they suffered the indignity of being sued, they may have believed, to varying degrees, that trial lawyers (without much differentiation between plaintiff and defense) were a menace to the practice of medicine and to their own practice. Now, with the receipt of a notice or suit, they are forced to deal with the menace. They feel wrongly attacked and defamed, pushed into an adversarial and defensive posture, and forced to cede control over their career and reputation to those very lawyers. There are several key aspects to this problem.

The Doctor Is Not in Control

Doctors are accustomed to situations where their mastery of the science and language of medicine places them firmly in control. It can be devastating to a doctor to learn how much of that goes out the window in litigation. The lawyer who is questioning the physician witness will be ready to challenge the witness, after having read the relevant literature, examined the chart with a fine-tooth comb, and consulted with his or her own expert. The questioner is not someone who is going to accept an answer, nod approvingly, and move on to the next question. As a witness, the physician has to accept these dynamics and understand that what counts in this situation is mastery of the science and the language of being a witness.

A physician witness can and should have a degree of control over the testimony, but it is control gained through process: slowing down, speaking carefully, being patient, not trying too hard, not answering poor questions, not guessing, and not volunteering information. So much of this is counterintuitive to physicians, or at least to their normal ways of communicating, that preparing them is a special challenge.

The Other Side Will Never Agree

Doctors are used to a problem-solving environment in which they work together, talk among themselves, and attempt to arrive at an agreement. Even if no agreement is reached, at the very least, the other side will listen and respect opinions. In a problem-solving environment, the goal is for all those involved to consider all facts and opinions in an unbiased way and then come to the best conclusion.

In litigation, it is hard for a doctor to understand that he or she is not going to persuade the other side that the care was appropriate. Doctors must understand that the constant attacks from the other side are not a reflection of the quality of care and they should not allow themselves to feel doubt or fear on the one hand or frustration or anger on the other. Patience and persistence are the only helpful responses: no matter how many times a question is asked or a challenge is raised, the answer remains the same.

The Job Is to Sell, Not to Solve

Doctors are used to talking about cases in an open, problem-solving manner, seeking the opinions of other professionals. They are used to an environment in which the goal is to come to a consensus on an appropriate course of action. In the witness environment, the other side has already come to a conclusion about what has happened. The lawyer who is doing the questioning has already reached his or her conclusion and has been hired by his or her side to be an advocate for that conclusion.

The doctor must understand that for better or worse, the search for truth here happens in a very different, noncollegial way, where the job is to convince the finder of fact of the appropriateness of the doctor's original decisions, not to explore the options. The physician witness has to understand that when providing testimony, it is not the witness's job to sell alternative theories. The selling is going to be done by the lawyers in opening and closing arguments, and most importantly, by the expert witnesses. When giving testimony, physicians must recognize that they are really talking to their own experts who are going to be reviewing the transcript along with the record in order to be able to make judgments about the case. The experts then sell that alternative explanation during trial. The doctor must have full faith in the process and understand that these points can be made, but not necessarily by the doctor.

2. Expertise

One of the hardest lessons for physician witnesses to learn is that their expertise, their background, and their good intentions are not dominant issues when it comes to trial. They must comprehend the tyranny of the "standard of care," experts, and treatises in litigation. The physician's intentions at the time of the care, however well meaning, take a back seat to the opinions of others who never met the patient.

In many cases, doctors have legitimately done or think they have done the best they can in treating a patient. Then they are suddenly confronted with the notion that their actions will be governed by an expert whom they have never met and whom the patient never met. Their actions will also be governed by literature that they may never have read. This becomes difficult for most physicians to understand and even more difficult for them to accept.

Realize That Doctors Cannot Be Their Own Experts

Both lawyers and doctors must understand the key role of outside experts from the very beginning of the case. Expert help is needed at the outset to help counsel anticipate the other side's approach and prepare the doctor on the standard of care. Then, the doctor must be made to understand—and come to terms with—the core role of the expert's views on standard of care throughout the case. It is the expert's opinion that will control or set the standard and not that of the physician witness.

Most physicians are accustomed to an entirely different process during their training. They are used to defending themselves during peer reviews and in front of inspection and quality assurance committees in hospitals. If they are called before a committee, they usually make their own case for their conduct. Therefore, when they approach the litigation process, they bring these same notions to the table. They still think that it is up to them, that they can be their own best expert, and that they will be able to explain or rationalize their conduct. What they need to understand is that it is much better in this context for somebody else to make the case for them. The physician's primary focus should be to be relentlessly polite and to demonstrate over and over again that he or she is caring, competent, and concerned. It is the lawyer and expert who must sell the rightness or wrongness of the physician's actions.

Understand the Role of Literature

The other key source for the standard of care, for both sides, is authoritative literature. With expert help, counsel must carefully assemble and review the relevant literature, and then prepare the physician witness on two issues. First, the physician witness must be careful about what is authoritative. This is a key concession in many states and many doctors are too quick to give it. In reality, they must be more careful with the question; medicine evolves, opinions differ even among experienced practitioners, and whether something is authoritative or not should reasonably depend on a variety of factors. Second, counsel, expert, and physician need to carefully consider the standard of care opinions in the literature and see how they fit the facts of the case.

Know the Record

There's no easier way for a doctor to be embarrassed or discredited than by failing to know the record. A properly prepared doctor has to know the record and understand the record and its flaws. If the physician witness does not know the chart, the jury may conclude that he or she doesn't really care about the case and probably didn't care about the patient at the

time of the treatment. Similarly, the doctor must know the deposition. Doctors don't always understand the significance of prior testimony or even of
minor contradictions. Nothing is more damning than changing the details
of the story as related at the deposition.

3. Ego

Doctors believe, often correctly, that they are smarter and better trained
in medicine than anyone involved in litigation: lawyers, judges, or juries.
Yet these are the people attacking and judging the doctor's professional
competence. The doctor must understand the artificiality of litigation: the
lawyer is not the real speaker, nor the real audience. Doctors are also used
to a professional language and to being the master of their conversations.
They now have to get used to speaking in an artificial setting in which the
language of question-and-answer and the discipline that accompanies it is
being imposed on them.

4. Emotions

Doctors are trained not to become emotional over other people's problems.
However, the flip side is that they have no professional experience being
emotional when it is their problem. They have a difficult time when their
professional life and professional integrity are, in their minds, challenged.
They get emotional about that and they don't know how to deal with it.
When personally sued, they may run the full gamut from fear to denial to
self-doubt to anger and back again. From a litigation perspective, it can
result in their going too far and being too definitive, or not going far enough
and being too defensive. Either extreme can be devastating. Adhering to
the Ten Rules becomes extremely important in this scenario, focusing particularly on the following issues:

Be Relentlessly Polite

This is a rule for all witnesses, but particularly here. Anger is a dangerous
distraction, and unpleasantness hurts the witness more than the questioner.
They are both luxuries the physician witness cannot afford. The witness
should be warned to never take a patronizing or sarcastic tone. Never argue
with the plaintiff's lawyer. Even a witness who wins a minor point still will

lose in the eyes of the jury if he or she is seen as argumentative or difficult. The goal is to come across as someone who is caring and sincere; you want each juror to think, "I would want this doctor to treat me and my family."

Avoid the Blame Game

With the finger of blame pointed at them, it is often tempting for doctors to try to deflect it elsewhere. Resist the temptation. Unless it has been discussed and agreed on as a clear strategy, finger-pointing usually benefits only plaintiff's counsel; everyone else looks bad.

Develop Trust

Lawyers should accept that doctors' distrust of our profession includes those who represent them. Take the time to develop a bond and a sense of trust. Take the time to explain that the approach that needs to be taken in this strange environment, while different and disturbing, is completely appropriate.

Be Wary of Appearance

No doctor wants to be told how to behave. Yet when venturing into this strange environment, physician witnesses should be told to look, act, and talk like the caring professionals they are, and the jury hopes for. Dress should be very neat and conservative. Attitudes should always be professional, caring, and respectful, especially when discussing patients. Failing to display a caring and professional attitude while giving testimony will create a negative impression in the minds of a jury and will lead them to conclude that the physician is not the caring professional they would hope to expect.

Keep It Simple

Having had their professional judgment or competence challenged, it is a natural reaction for doctors to want to overcompensate by trying to impress everyone with their testimony. Remember two things: keep it simple and don't volunteer. Proper testimony follows a somewhat stilted pattern of question, pause, answer, stop. There are no shortcuts. Follow that slow, steady rhythm. Also, speak plain English; avoid complicated medical jargon, and when you must use it, explain in lay terms as well. Finally, be wary of hypothetical questions; they are often meant to trap, not spur, academic discourse.

Remember—This Is Not a Conversation

Part of the artificiality of a deposition is that the opposing lawyer is not really the one asking the questions, or the one to whom the doctor is speaking. The questions have presumably been supplied by the plaintiff's experts, the literature, or other sources. The answers are for the benefit of the most important person in the room—the court reporter, who will take down every word so that it can be picked apart using all the same expert sources. Doctors must understand that by testifying, they are dictating the first and final draft of one of the most important documents of their professional career. Care and caution are the watchwords.

The practice of medicine does not translate well into the practice of tort litigation: these are not peers working together; the focus is on assigning blame retrospectively, not solving problems prospectively, and the search for truth, to whatever extent either profession is truly engaged in it, is through a completely foreign and arbitrary process. The various conflicts between professional characteristics and the circumstances of litigation turn many good doctors into poor witnesses. It is our responsibility as counsel to recognize these conflicts, help the physician witness recognize them, and then find the considerable time and energy required to confront the challenge of preparing a doctor on both the substance and process of being a witness.

Chapter 33

The Criminal Defendant

Another key distinction among types of proceedings is between civil and criminal matters. Reduced to the most basic level, the difference is jail. A civil matter, whether litigation, administrative, or any other kind, can result in money damages or fines, and orders for what individuals or entities can or cannot do. A criminal matter can result in all of this, plus a criminal conviction and the possibility of imprisonment.

There are many differences in procedures; for example, police and a grand jury enter into a criminal investigation, and a criminal defendant has a right to a jury trial. However, one of the most significant differences is that in a criminal matter (or any matter in which there are potential criminal implications), the witness has a constitutional right not to be forced to testify. This right appears in most state constitutions, but it is most commonly referred to by its location in the Constitution: the Fifth Amendment.

What the Fifth Amendment says is this: "No person . . . shall be compelled in any criminal case to be a witness against himself." What it means is that while you can willingly say something that gets you into trouble, you cannot be forced to do so. The witness can almost always refuse to answer a question on the grounds that a truthful answer "may tend to incriminate me."

People are sometimes reluctant to use this right out of concern that it means they are saying they did something wrong or that it will be viewed as such. In a civil case this may be true, because a jury may hear of a witness's assertion of Fifth Amendment rights and be allowed to draw inferences against the witness based on it. However, in a criminal case, from a legal perspective, the following conditions apply:

1. The decision to exercise this important constitutional right cannot be used against a witness or even mentioned to the jury.
2. The scope of criminal law has greatly expanded over the years, now including broad concepts of conspiracy, regulatory offenses, and other acts not previously viewed as criminal, so the scope of a witness's possible exposure has broadened as well.
3. The law is clear that this right protects the innocent as well as the guilty, and what the government may see as incriminating is far broader than a traditional confession.

What all this means is that any time a client may be a witness in any matter, you and your client have to decide whether he or she should go forward or exercise the right not to speak. That can be an easy decision, one way or the other, or a very difficult cost/ benefit balancing, depending on a number of questions, including:

- What are the risks and advantages of speaking?
- What new information would be disclosed?
- How effective an explanation can be given for the case the government (or opponent, in a civil case) already has?

Reasons to Have a Criminal Defendant Testify

There is a common notion that it is wise not to put a criminal defendant on the stand, barring some earthquake or other natural disaster. As a general guide, that makes good sense. However, sometimes, as lawyers, we tend to rely on this notion as a crutch instead of a guide. Consequently, only a small percentage of defendants actually take the stand. As lawyers, we often tend to substitute this conventional wisdom for a defendant's decision not to take the stand. It is important to remember that there are no absolutes in this business, and, in fact, putting certain criminal defendants on the witness stand can present opportunities to further your case. The two principal reasons to take advantage of these opportunities are that: (1) the jury wants to hear the defendant's testimony and (2) the defendant wants to testify.

The Jury Wants to Hear It

Juries are instructed that criminal defendants have no obligation to put on any evidence. I believe in juries. They try to follow a judge's instructions. When the judge tells them that they cannot take into account the fact that the defendant did not take the stand, they believe it in their heads and understand it. However, in their hearts, they want to hear the defendant's testimony. They wonder, "If he is really innocent, why doesn't he take the stand?" They want to see the defendant take the stand and deny the charges, even though he or she is not obligated to do so. This unspoken assumption is difficult to overcome. Putting certain criminal defendants on the stand counteracts this assumption.

The Defendant Wants to Say It

In many cases, the defendant wants to take the stand. While this may not be advisable in some situations, we need to make an effort to respect the client's desires. As lawyers, we are giving advice, but the client's desires are also a significant consideration and cannot be ignored. There are several obstacles and considerations that must be taken into account before deciding to put the defendant on the stand:

- *Guilt or Innocence.* If you know your client committed the crime, it is more difficult to put him or her on the stand. If you know your client did not commit the crime, this may or may not make the decision easier.
- *Baggage.* Regardless of guilt or innocence, if the client has lots of baggage, either related to the crime or unrelated but admissible if he or she takes the stand, then this will have an effect on your decision. For example, if you put the client on the stand, will a prior conviction come in? Are unrelated acts going to become admissible?
- *Ability.* People differ in their ability to testify. Before putting a criminal defendant on the stand, you have to evaluate the client's ability to express himself or herself. This does not just mean how articulate or well-spoken the client is; it is a determination of how he or she comes across. Will the jury believe your client? This is an important consideration because if the jury believes your client is lying on the stand, none of the other evidence will matter. You can turn a very close case

for the prosecution into a slam-dunk for them by having a client who *appears* to be lying, even if he or she is telling the truth.

- *Desire.* Whether the defendant wants to take the stand or not is also an important consideration. A defendant who thinks taking the stand is abhorrent is not likely to make a good witness.

Deciding whether or not to place a criminal defendant on the stand involves weighing many critical factors. There is no way to make the decision properly without full and candid discussions with your client. The interplay of legal and factual issues can be complicated and uncertain. As a result, the decision may be easy or hard, but in any event, it should not be made out of ignorance.

Chapter 34

The Ethics of Witness Preparation

"The lawyer's duty is to extract the facts from the witness, not to pour them into him; to learn what the witness does know, not to teach him what he ought to know."

—*In re Eldridge*, 37 N.Y. 161, 171 (N.Y. 1880)

The question of what constitutes ethical witness preparation is one that, as the saying goes, has generated much heat but little light. A few academics have taken the extreme route, arguing that *any* witness preparation distorts the search for truth, and is therefore improper. *See, e.g.*, R. Wydick, *The Ethics of Witness Coaching*, 17 CARDOZO L. REV. 1 (1995) ("If a trial is supposed to be a search for truth, why then are lawyers allowed to interview and prepare witnesses?")

However, with all due respect to the Ivory Tower, that is an absurd position. Witness preparation is all about leveling the playing field: the questioner is experienced in this strange and unnatural process, skilled in turning every careless word to his or her advantage, familiar with all sides and all aspects of the case, and perhaps most importantly, infallible: no matter how many mistakes the questioner makes, it doesn't matter. The questioner is not under oath. Yet just one mistake by a witness can severely damage his or her credibility or case, and can live on forever. What could be more unfair? How can lawyers fulfill their obligation to represent clients "zealously within the bounds of the law" (Model Code, EC7-1), and allow this to happen? They cannot. The great legal scholar John Wigmore recognized "[t]he absolute necessity of such a [witness preparation] conference for legitimate purposes." 3 WIGMORE ON EVIDENCE § 788 (3d ed. [1940]). The challenge, then, is not whether to prepare witnesses, but how.

A relative of mine is an author. She creates wonderful works of fiction, from her own experiences and imagination. Some of those creations then get translated into other languages, for readers around the world. Since I know little about languages, I had the notion that translating is a mechanical process; after all, we can go online to get words or phrases translated from a long list of languages. But when the material is more complex, more nuanced, and more colloquial, like a work of fiction, the translator's task is very different. My relative receives a steady stream of correspondence from translators around the world, some of it quite funny, asking for help in understanding slang, sayings, and other creative uses of language. What does a certain phrase mean, and how and why is it being used here?

The translator's task is very different from the author's. The translator is not creating new material—he or she is taking that material and making it understandable in another language. That may require suggesting new phrasing where comparable words don't exist, new analogies or colloquialisms where the original would not be readily comprehensible, and various other changes. But the essential creation remains the same even though it is appearing in a new language.

So it is with witness preparation. The witness is the author, the creator of the material. The lawyer is the translator, helping the witness to communicate that material in a strange language, rhythm, and environment, but the lawyer is not creating new material. As Chief Justice Burger observed when considering the dynamics of witness preparation, "[A]n attorney must respect the important distinction between discussing testimony and seeking to improperly influence it." *Geders v. United States*, 425 U.S. 80, 89 n.3 (1976). However, finding that line between creating and translating is not always easy.

The key is to emphasize to the witness, right from the start, the importance of Rule 3: Tell the Truth. That is the principal guidance that the ethical rules give on this topic. Disciplinary Rule 7-102(A) of the Model Code of Professional Responsibility states that a lawyer "shall not . . . participate in the creation or preservation of evidence when he knows or it is obvious that the evidence is false" and shall not "counsel or assist his client in conduct that the lawyer knows to be illegal or fraudulent." The witness needs to clearly and unequivocally understand that counsel is seeking no more—and no less—than the truth.

With that essential foundation, effective witness preparation can—and must—go forward. "A lawyer who did not prepare his or her witness for testimony, having had an opportunity to do so, would not be doing his or her professional job properly." District of Columbia Bar, Ethics Opinion No. 79 (1979), p. 139. One author put it a little more bluntly: "It is probably unethical to fail to prepare a witness, and it is undoubtedly cruel to subject anyone to cross-examination without preparation." David Berg, *Preparing Witnesses*, LITIGATION 14 (Winter 1987).

As long as it is focused on developing and clarifying truthful testimony, such preparation may include the lawyer:

- being "persistent and aggressive in presenting [counsel's] theory of the case" (*RTC v. Bright*, 6 F.3d 336, 342 (5th Cir. 1993));
- suggesting language to the witness that may aid the testimony (D.C. Bar Legal Ethics Comm., Op. 79 at 139 (1979));
- suggesting substantive points to the witness (D.C. Bar Legal Ethics Comm., Op. 79 at 139 (1979)); and
- conducting "practice examination or cross-examination" (D.C. Bar Legal Ethics Comm., Op. 79 at 140 (1979)).

What Can You Do?

In preparing a witness to testify, a lawyer is permitted to invite the witness to provide truthful testimony that is favorable to the lawyer's client, as long as the lawyer does not encourage the witness to deviate from the truth. The Restatement of the Law Governing Lawyers provides that as long as it does not elicit false or misleading testimony, preparation consistent with a lawyer's duties to a client and to the court may include:

1. discussing the role of the witness and effective courtroom demeanor;
2. discussing the witness's recollection and probable testimony;

3. revealing to the witness other testimony or evidence that will be presented and asking the witness to reconsider his or her recollection or recounting of events in that light;
4. discussing the applicability of law to the events at issue;
5. reviewing the factual context into which the witness's observations or opinions will fit;
6. reviewing documents or other physical evidence that may be introduced;
7. discussing probable lines of hostile cross-examination that the witness should be prepared to meet; and
8. practicing the witness's testimony and suggesting choice of words.

Both the witness and the lawyer share a responsibility for ensuring the truth of the witness's testimony. This means that the witness should never testify to something he or she does not believe to be true. Additionally, as a lawyer, you should never permit the witness to testify to what you, as the lawyer, believe to be false. A belief that the witness's testimony is false should be based on personal knowledge or have a firm factual basis. This exists when "facts known to the lawyer or the client's own statements indicate that the testimony is false." (RESTATEMENT OF THE LAW GOVERNING LAWYERS § 120.) Ethical witness preparation must be controlled by these fundamental obligations.

The Perjury Dilemma

The classic problem in ethical witness preparation is the perjury dilemma: the client who intends to lie, or has done so. It is a dilemma caused by the conflict that situation creates between a lawyer's obligation to preserve client confidences (e.g., Model Code of Professional Responsibility, DR 4-101), and the obligation to preserve the court's integrity (e.g., Model Code of Professional Responsibility, DR 7-102). The search for a way out of this dilemma has, over time, involved what I call the Four Horsemen of the Lying Witness Apocalypse: persuasion, narrative, withdrawal, and disclosure.

1. Persuasion

Without question, counsel has an obligation to try vigorously to persuade the client to tell the truth. As the Supreme Court has stated, "the right to counsel includes no right to have a lawyer who will cooperate with planned perjury." *Nix v. Whiteside*, 479 U.S. 197 (1986).

2. Narrative

The once-fashionable idea was that lawyers could minimize the dilemma by minimizing their involvement: just put the witness on the stand, and let him or her tell a narrative without questions or other "help" from counsel. However, this is an endless minefield: how does counsel present or argue the case, and are we simply rewarding more articulate liars who may need less "help"?

3. Withdrawal

A popular view for a time was that the last best resort for counsel would be to withdraw from the case. However, the true dangers of perjured testimony are *not* for counsel—they are for the courts, the system, and the public. Counsel's withdrawal does not lessen the danger; in fact, it may increase it. The witness may simply find more willing counsel, or not be as open with new counsel, and thereby increase the likelihood that the courts will be relying on false testimony. Withdrawal, alas, is a false remedy.

4. Disclosure

The power of privilege is so strong that disclosure to the tribunal was once largely a "thou shalt not." But recognizing the failure of the other approaches, it is becoming viewed more favorably. For example, a fairly recent New York ethics opinion stated: "A lawyer who comes to know that a client has lied about a material issue in a deposition . . . must . . . if necessary, disclos(e) to the tribunal." (N.Y. County Lawyers Ass'n, Ethics Op. 741 (2010).) It's a treacherous world out there. If you think you have a perjury dilemma, then think, document, read, and consult before you act.

Lawyer Conduct during a Deposition

The limitations on what a lawyer can say and do during a deposition vary among jurisdictions. As a general rule, lawyers are supposed to conduct themselves at depositions with the same formality and solemnity that is mandated in the courtroom. A lawyer may be sanctioned for displaying inappropriate behavior, such as attempting to interrupt the deposition by interjecting nonexistent privileges and instructing the witness not to answer a question without having a good-faith basis. Rule 30(d)(2) of the Federal Rules of Civil Procedure allows sanctions against anyone who "impedes, delays, or frustrates the fair examination of the deponent." This may include the following:

Speaking Objections. The Federal Rules require that "[a]n objection must be stated concisely in a nonargumentative and nonsuggestive manner." FED. R. CIV. P. 30(c)(2). For example, the Florida Rules of Court prohibit "objections or statements which have the effect of coaching the witness, instructing the witness concerning the way in which he or she should frame a response, or suggesting an answer to the witness." (S.D. Fla. L.R., Gen. Rule 30.1). In one case, for example, sanctions were imposed for counsel's repeated statement that "I don't think she understands what you mean," and other speaking objections. *Cholfin v. Gordon,* 1995 WL 809916 (Mass. 1995).

Instructions Not to Answer. The Advisory Committee Notes to the Federal Civil Rules state, "Directions to a deponent not to answer a question can be even more disruptive than objections." As a result, the rules—and the courts—are stricter than what some counsel practice. "A person may instruct a deponent not to answer only when necessary to preserve a privilege, to enforce a limitation ordered by the Court, or to present a motion under Rule 30(d)(3)." FED. R. CIV. P. 30(c)(2).

Conferences with Counsel. Courts have struggled more with limitations on—and abuses of—conferences with counsel. In one of the most often-cited cases on this issue, a court in Pennsylvania found that lawyer and client do not have an absolute right to privately confer during the course of the client's deposition. (*Hall v. Clifton Precision,* 150 F.R.D. 525, 528 (E.D. Pa. 1993)). ("I hold that conferences between witness and lawyer are prohibited both during the deposition and during recesses.") In *Plaisted v. Geisinger*

Medical Center, 210 F.R.D. 527 (M.D. Pa. 2002), the court stated it would "adopt the guidelines for attorney behaviour at depositions announced in Hall." *Id.*, at 522. Based on those guidelines, the court allowed "plaintiffs' counsel to pose questions to [defendant's employee] about any discussion that may have taken place during the two breaks defense counsel improperly took during his deposition." *Id.*, at 535.

However, "several cases have held that the Hall case goes too far . . . [and] . . . declined to adopt the Hall court's 'strict requirements.'" *Murray v. Nationwide Better Health*, 2012 WL 3683397 (C.D. Ill. 2012). Conferences while a question is pending are universally prohibited unless they are conducted to protect a privilege. Beyond that, courts have tried to balance the competing considerations. For example, one court found that a prohibition on conferences during breaks, "is appropriate and customary during the actual deposition," but refused to extend it over a multiple-day deposition. *United States v. Phillip Morris*, 212 F.R.D. 418 (D.C. 2002). *See McDermott v. Miami Dade County*, 753 So. 2d 729 (1st Dist. Fla. 2000) (precluding a lawyer from conferring with his client about details of her alleged injury after the lawyer improperly interrupted the deposition).

Because of the varying rules governing attorney conduct during a deposition, every practitioner must be knowledgeable on the rules in his or her jurisdiction. In order to protect oneself from court sanctions and protect the integrity of the legal system, a lawyer should be knowledgeable about these rules because they will have a significant effect on the extent of preparation that will be necessary. They will help both the witness and the lawyer anticipate problems that may arise during the course of the deposition and/or proceeding and prepare accordingly.

Over 50 years ago, one court recognized that "[i]t is usual and legitimate practice for ethical and diligent counsel to confer with a witness whom he is about to call prior to his giving testimony." *Homdi v. Fire Association of Philadelphia*, 20 F.R.D. 181, 182 (S.D.N.Y. 1957). However, recognizing the importance of witness preparation also means appreciating its challenges.

Chapter 35

The Witness Bill of Rights

When I spoke in chapter 8, "Preparing Ourselves," of the challenges of preparation that lawyers face, I referenced the Three Cs: control, credibility, and confidence. The Ten Rules teach a discipline that helps a witness establish control and credibility. Hopefully, they lead to confidence, but for many witnesses that can be a far more elusive goal. So much is being required of them that they may feel overwhelmed. They may feel that everyone seems to have rights and powers except them. It's a downward spiral; some degree of confidence is vital for control and credibility, and vice versa.

For such witnesses, as a reward for the hard work of preparation, I have with flair and flourish handed them the Witness Bill of Rights, which simply takes the ten instructive rules and turns them into ten affirmative rights. These are not legal rights formally set forth in some statute or case. Rather, they are based on fairness and common courtesy. I call them rights because the witness must demand them—the witness must require them from the questioner through these rules. Few questioners will offer them unbidden. These rights, with brief explanations, are set forth next.

1. You Have the Right to Control the Pace of Your Testimony

(Rule 1: Take Your Time.) This is the essential foundation for clear, fair, truthful testimony. Anything else is grossly unfair to the witness. Control the pace; slow down.

2. You Have the Right to Question the Questioner

(Rule 2: Remember You Are Making a Record.) This is your testimony, so don't let someone else put words in your mouth. Words can have different meanings in jargon, in legalese, and in English. If you are not 100 percent certain of, and comfortable with, how the questioner is using a word or phrase, you cannot answer the question.

3. You Have the Right to Tell Your Story

(Rule 3: Tell the Truth.) It's your truth, not the questioner's. It includes good stuff, bad stuff, mistakes, and rough edges. It does not include anything beyond what you saw, heard, or did.

4. You Have the Right to Be Treated with Respect

(Rule 4: Be Relentlessly Polite.) Do not dignify a questioner's garbage questions, sarcasm, or nasty attitude by lowering yourself to that level. Stay cool, calm, positive, and relentlessly polite. Good testimony is the best revenge.

5. You Have the Right to Clear and Fair Questions

(Rule 5: Don't Answer a Question You Don't Understand.) Whatever the reason—whether it's related to clarity, comprehension, or comfort—if you don't fully understand a question, say so. You need only say "Please rephrase the question." Don't let the questioner wiggle and squirm out of that discipline. Insist on clear and fair questions.

6. You Have the Right to Forget

(Rule 6: If You Don't Remember, Say So.) The long gap between the events in question and when you're being asked questions about them is not your fault. Nor is this a test at school, where you will be penalized for forgetting. Just say "I don't recall" as often as you need to.

7. You Have the Right to Make Clear What You Don't Know

(Rule 7: Don't Guess.) It's the curse of the intelligent witness—having no experience or comfort in making clear what you don't know. But being able to do so is essential here. Whether it involves factual details, inferences, or hypotheticals, being 95 percent sure isn't good enough in this precise environment. If you're not 100 percent certain, then it's a guess. Don't guess.

8. You Have the Right to Silence

(Rule 8: Don't Volunteer.) Question, pause, answer, stop. You don't have to do the questioner's job, and help ask the next question, fill in the gaps, or go where you think the questioner wants to. Get comfortable with uncomfortable silence.

9. You Have the Right to See and Read All Documents

(Rule 9: Be Careful with Documents and Prior Statements.) Credibility, language, and context: those are the issues. There is no magic to documents. If you didn't write it *and* you don't remember it, there is little you can say about it. Ask to see the document, read it carefully, ask for the question again, consider whether the document has been quoted accurately and in context, then consider whether you really have anything to add to what's on paper.

10. You Have the Right to Use Your Counsel

(Rule 10: Use Your Counsel.) Understand the importance of the Ten Rules, of objections, and of breaks. Use what you have learned to impose rules, discipline, and ultimately, control, on the process.

Chapter 36

Conclusion

The process we've just described has three basic goals: (1) to level the playing field; (2) to allow the witness to take control; and, (3) to tell our story. The witness environment is an extraordinarily deceptive one, in that it has all the *appearances* of the questioner being in control. It is the questioner's subpoena, court or conference room, and questions. You must explain to witnesses that if they accept that notion, they lose. Because despite all appearances of the questioner being in control, the whole point of the exercise is to get the witnesses' testimony. Because of this, the witness has a right to take control, not in an adversarial way, but in a very simple way, by following the basic rules laid out in this book.

Some years ago, a colleague of mine asked for my help in a divorce case. His client, the wife, had testified in a deposition for one day but had not finished and was now scheduled for a second day. However, my colleague was on trial in another case, had already had to postpone this second day of deposition several times, and was afraid that the court would not give him another extension (opposing counsel had already refused). Would I step in on short notice and represent her at the continued deposition?

When I read the transcript of the prior deposition, I was disheartened. Here was an obviously intelligent, honest, caring person who had nevertheless been a disaster as a witness. The marriage and divorce were both ugly. The husband had been mentally abusive and domineering during the marriage. She had responded by always trying to "fix" things, by being ever nicer and ever more helpful, until her husband finally left her. Both of their characteristics carried over into the divorce and depositions. The husband had hired an old family friend as his lawyer, which devastated her, and had then pushed the lawyer to play hardball at every turn.

Worse still, in her deposition testimony, she was still trying to fix this mess by being helpful, and by trying to give them what she thought they wanted. In doing so, she had committed all the classic witness mistakes: she tried too hard, she didn't listen carefully, she talked too much, and she was totally undisciplined and imprecise in her answers. Mostly, she just talked too fast; between her nervousness and her giving nature, she couldn't wait to try to be helpful.

I was not easy on her when we first met. I told her that she was not going to fix this difficult litigation by being too nice in a deposition; she was only going to give the other side the ammunition to abuse her more. She was an intelligent, mature woman who had been taken advantage of in a bad marriage and was now going to be taken advantage of in a bad divorce, if she did not take control of her future. The first step toward taking control of her future was to take control of this deposition. The first step toward doing that was to slow down.

We went at length through all the rules in this book: don't guess, don't volunteer, and so on. However, the one we kept coming back to was Rule 1: Take your time. The need to regain control of the process was so dramatic that we clearly had to focus on building a strong foundation with this rule. It was so important that we did it mechanically: Count to five in your head after every question. Over and over, I insisted on that discipline in preparation. The mock deposition left her repeatedly in tears. Changing old habits is hard in the best of circumstances, but it was much more so here.

By the time of the deposition, I knew that she understood the rules intellectually. Still, I was not sure that she could pull it off emotionally. When we walked into opposing counsel's conference room, both the husband and his lawyer were there and clearly feeling good. Why shouldn't they? The first day had gone so well for them that perhaps they thought the second day would probably be even more fun. If they could have sold popcorn for the event, they would have.

We were all in for a surprise. Human nature is such that most of us are stronger than we—or others—give us credit for. Often, we can rise to great challenges if we put our heads and our hearts into it. My client had found that strength, and the result was extraordinary. From the very first request ("Please state your name."), she sat up firmly and politely in her chair with hands folded in her lap, looked the questioner straight in the eye, counted slowly to five in her head, gave the simplest possible answer ("Anne"), and then stopped and waited for the next question.

By the time she had done this same thing for the first several questions in a row, everyone in the room (yes, I confess, including me) was stunned. When she kept at it consistently for the first hour, the husband's lawyer was clearly in trouble. What many witnesses—*and lawyers*—don't realize is that just as anyone can be a bad witness if they are not prepared, anyone can *question* a bad witness without much effort or preparation. Questioning a witness who is prepared and disciplined is far more difficult, and at the very least requires a much higher level of preparation and discipline by the questioner. This lawyer (like many questioners) was neither capable nor prepared enough to deal with this new, highly disciplined witness.

Through four hours of testimony, she remained consistent: polite, firm, well-paced, and precise. After two hours, the husband's lawyer was literally squirming with discomfort. By the end, it was clear to all (including the husband) that the deposition, as an effort to get her to say things they could later use against her, had been a complete failure. She had given them nothing to work with and had fixed many of the problems of the first round. We walked out in quiet triumph, with my client still being her demure, refined self. Out in the parking lot, though, she shrieked with joy, flung her arms around me, and exclaimed, "That's the first time in 25 years that I've been in control of that son of a bitch!"

What had she done? She took her time, she followed the rules, and she took control. There was no magic to it, just hard work and concentration. Any witness can do it—but not without your help.

Appendix A

Sample Witness Outline

Capt. Smith 5. Ship's Log	
1990—Captain: Flying Dove Fishing Grand Banks Responsible: ship's document	(Depo., p. 187, 1.6)
Log—Important Required by Coast Guard —Captain Responsible Records tip	(38 C.F.R. 1089)
Flying Dove Log — Handwriting— Accurate —Feb. 3, 1990	(Exhibit 37) —Offer (Exh. 37, p. 38)

Bismark v. *Titanic*, 508 F.2d 193, 198 (21st Cir. 1991) ("Commercial ship's log is a business record if kept in the ordinary course. . . .")

Appendix B

Witness Preparation Summary Handout

Discussion

For a number of years, I have used a memorandum containing a brief overview of the proceeding and a summary of the Ten Rules to help witnesses in their preparation. The next section of this appendix contains a series of alternate introductions, containing similar language but different overviews for a variety of proceedings. The third section of the appendix contains a summary of the Ten Rules. By putting together the appropriate introduction and the rules text, you can create the summary memo for witnesses. It will give you the option of using either the book as a whole, or the summary memo, or both, for preparation, depending on the nature of the client and the matter.

The best way to use the memo is not to send it to the client and then just ignore it. It is far more useful as an integrated part of the preparation process. I usually wait until I have met with the client, gone over the facts briefly, and discussed the importance of preparation in that context. I then give the client the memo and ask him or her to read it carefully, jotting down right on the document any thoughts or questions it raises, so that we can use it as the basis for our next meeting.

At the next preparation session, I will tactfully try to find out whether the client has read the memo. However, whether or not the client has read the memo carefully, I will still walk through it with them, trying to tie the rules to that case. I then refer back to the memo, and the rules, at every subsequent stage of preparation.

Introductions

Deposition

You have been called as a witness in a deposition in a civil case. A deposition consists primarily of questions by lawyers and your answers, under oath, transcribed by a court reporter, with your lawyer present. A deposition is *not* a trial. There is no judge or jury present, and nobody is there to keep score or award a verdict. Charm, persuasiveness, sincerity, and other appealing human attributes are largely wasted in a deposition. The result is a written record known as a transcript, which will be used (or misused) by the lawyers when the actual trial occurs. Therefore, the most important task for a witness in a deposition is to keep the transcript clear and accurate.

Although it often has some of the appearances of informality—a conference room setting, a casual atmosphere among counsel—a deposition is a difficult, often artificial and unnatural procedure that demands your careful attention and preparation. The notion that you can just go in and tell your story without intensive preparation is an invitation to disaster. This memorandum is intended to help you *begin* the process of preparation. Please study it, think about it, and use it as a basis for asking questions when you meet with counsel.

The oath you will take at the beginning of the deposition is to tell the truth, the whole truth, and nothing but the truth. Like many things in our normal lives, we tend to blur it all together into one image. Like many things in the precise and artificial world of a deposition, you need to examine the *entire* statement, and make sure that you understand and seriously consider all three parts. There are, after all, three parts to the oath for good reasons.

In a deposition, the hardest part of following your oath is to tell nothing but the truth. This takes a surprising amount of preparation, concentration, and internal discipline. Much of what we do or say to keep a normal, casual conversation going must be avoided at a deposition. In friendly conversation, to avoid looking rude, or foolish, or uninformed, we often embellish or shade our knowledge or understanding in perfectly innocent and acceptable ways: We guess, we assume, we hide our lack of memory or knowledge, we gossip, we draw inferences, we talk too much, and we speak without careful thinking. Changing these typical habits is hard work, but it is *essential* for a successful deposition.

Two basic principles should guide you in this effort. The first is that it has often been said that the three most important rules for any witness are "listen, listen, and listen." To respond appropriately and precisely, you must listen to every word of every question with a focus and discipline that none of us use in our normal conversations. The second basic principle sounds even simpler, but it is actually very hard to achieve. Most witnesses get into difficulty not because they are trying to lie but rather because they are trying *too hard* to tell the truth. As a result, they end up going beyond what they truly know or remember. So the other principle is simply "don't try too hard." The Ten Rules that follow are really just guides to help you put these two principles into practice.

Interview

The government has asked to interview you on the matters we've discussed. The interview will involve the two of us meeting with one or more government agents/investigators, and possibly one or more government lawyers. You will probably be asked questions on your background, your work, and a variety of other matters, as well as the subject matter of the inquiry. The investigators will be taking notes.

This will be an informal interview, in the sense that there is no judge or jury, and it will not be formally recorded or transcribed. Do not be fooled by the informality. This is a very serious, and sometimes risky, process. *Every* question from the government, no matter how friendly, has a purpose. *Every* statement by you, no matter how casual, may be written down and used. It is a difficult, often artificial, and unnatural procedure that demands your careful attention and preparation. The notion that you can just go in and tell your story without intensive preparation is an invitation to disaster. This memorandum is intended to help you *begin* the process of preparation. Please study it, think about it, and use it as a basis for asking questions when we meet.

Although the interview is not "sworn" (you will not take an oath), you should treat it as if you *were* under oath. Lying in an interview like this is foolish and dangerous. It can be used against you in various ways, possibly including criminal prosecution. Treat it as *if* you had taken an oath to tell the truth, the whole truth, and nothing but the truth. Like many things in our normal lives, we tend to blur it all together into one image. Like many things in the precise and artificial world of an interview, you need to examine the *entire* statement, and make sure that you understand and seriously consider all three parts. There are, after all, three parts to the oath for good reasons.

In an interview, the hardest part of following the oath is to tell nothing but the truth. This takes a surprising amount of preparation, concentration, and internal discipline. Much of what we do or say to keep a normal, casual conversation going must be avoided. In friendly conversation, to avoid looking rude, or foolish, or uninformed, we often embellish or shade our knowledge or understanding in perfectly innocent and acceptable ways. We guess, we assume, we hide our lack of memory or knowledge, we gossip, we talk too much, and we speak without careful thinking. Changing these typical habits is hard work, but it is *essential* for a successful interview.

Two basic principles should guide you in this effort. The first is that it has often been said that the three most important rules for any witness are "listen, listen, and listen." To respond appropriately and precisely, you must listen to every word of every question with a focus and discipline that none of us use in our normal conversation. The second basic principle sounds even simpler, but it is actually very hard to achieve. Most witnesses get into difficulty not because they are trying to lie but rather because they are trying *too hard* to tell the truth. As a result, they end up going beyond what they truly know or remember. So the other principle is simply "don't try too hard." The Ten Rules that follow are really just guides to help you put these two principles into practice.

Government Agency Testimony

[NB: Circumstances may vary among different agencies.]

You have been called to testify as a witness before the [ABC Government Agency (ABC)]. This will consist primarily of questions by an ABC lawyer/

investigator and your answers, under oath, transcribed by a court reporter, with me present as your lawyer. You will probably be asked questions on your background, your work, and a variety of other matters, as well as the subject matter of the inquiry. This is *not* a trial. No judge or jury is present, and nobody is there to keep score or award a verdict. The result is a written record known as a transcript, which may be used (or misused) by the lawyers in later proceedings. Therefore, the most important task for a witness is to keep the transcript clear and accurate.

Although it may have some of the appearances of informality—a conference room setting, a casual atmosphere among counsel—this is a difficult, often artificial, and unnatural procedure that demands your careful attention and preparation. The notion that you can just go in and tell your story without intensive preparation is an invitation to disaster. This memorandum is intended to help you *begin* the process of preparation. Please study it, think about it, and use it as a basis for asking questions when we meet.

The oath you will take at the beginning of your testimony is to tell the truth, the whole truth, and nothing but the truth. Like many things in our normal lives, we tend to blur it all together into one image. Like many things in the precise and artificial world of ABC testimony, you need to examine the *entire* statement, and make sure that you understand and seriously consider all three parts. There are, after all, three parts to the oath for good reasons.

Usually, the hardest part of following your oath is to tell nothing but the truth. This takes a surprising amount of preparation, concentration, and internal discipline. Much of what we do or say to keep a normal, casual conversation going must be avoided. In friendly conversation, to avoid looking rude, or foolish, or uninformed, we often embellish or shade our knowledge or understanding in perfectly innocent and acceptable ways. We guess, we assume, we hide our lack of memory or knowledge, we gossip, we talk too much, and we speak without careful thinking. Changing these typical habits is hard work, but it is *essential* for successful testimony.

Two basic principles should guide you in this effort. The first is that it has often been said that the three most important rules for any witness are "listen, listen, and listen." To respond appropriately and precisely, you must listen to every word of every question with a focus and discipline that none of us use in our normal conversations. The second basic principle sounds even simpler, but it is actually very hard to achieve. Most witnesses get into difficulty not because they are trying to lie, but rather because they are trying *too hard* to tell the truth. As a result, they end up going beyond what they truly know or remember. So the other principle is simply "don't try too hard." The Ten Rules that follow are really just guides to help you put these two principles into practice.

Grand Jury Testimony (Federal)

You have been subpoenaed to appear as a witness before a federal grand jury. This is a very serious proceeding, and it can be a frightening and confusing prospect for most people. This memo is intended to help you understand this process and the difficult but critical job of preparing for your appearance. Please read it carefully, and bring any questions or thoughts that it raises with you when we meet to prepare.

A federal grand jury is a group of 16 to 23 people, chosen at random, who come together to hear evidence and decide whether there is "probable cause" to believe that someone has committed a crime. The grand jury has broad powers to compel people to testify or produce documents. Witnesses testify under oath, the testimony is transcribed by a court reporter, and after hearing testimony and receiving documents the grand jury may vote on whether or not to bring ("return") formal criminal charges (an "indictment").

The grand jury is an important part of our system of justice, but it is important for a witness to realize that it is neither an open nor an even process. It is not "open" because grand jury proceedings are secret. Only the grand jurors, the prosecutor, the court reporter, and the witnesses are allowed in the room. Even the witness's counsel must stay outside (but you can come out to talk as often as you like). Everyone involved—*except* the witness and his or her counsel—is supposed to keep the proceedings secret.

The grand jury is not "even" because the prosecutor has enormous control over the process. In reality, the prosecutor generally decides who or what the grand jury will investigate, who will appear before them including what witnesses or documents will be subpoenaed, what questions will be asked, and what indictments will be drafted and presented. The prosecutor is under no obligation to present "both sides of the story."

If all this sounds one-sided, it *is*, and that can make it difficult. Witnesses are not without rights: You have a Fifth Amendment right not to incriminate yourself (if you do not already have immunity), an absolute right to consult with counsel at all times, and other rights. However, your most important protection is often careful preparation with counsel. The notion that you can just go in and tell your story in this new and strange environment without intensive preparation is an invitation to disaster.

The oath you will take at the beginning of the grand jury is to tell the truth, the whole truth, and nothing but the truth. Like many things in our normal lives, we tend to blur it all together into one image. Like many things in the precise and artificial world of giving testimony, you need to examine the *entire* statement, and make sure that you understand and seriously consider all three parts. There are, after all, three parts to the oath for good reasons.

In the grand jury, the hardest part of following your oath is to tell nothing but the truth. This takes a surprising amount of preparation, concentration, and internal discipline. Much of what we do or say to keep a normal, casual conversation going must be avoided at a grand jury. In friendly conversation, to avoid looking rude, or foolish, or uninformed, we often embellish or shade our knowledge or understanding in perfectly innocent and acceptable ways. We guess, we assume, we hide our lack of memory or knowledge, we gossip, we talk too much, and we speak without careful thinking. Changing these typical habits is hard work, but it is *essential* for successful testimony.

Two basic principles should guide you in this effort. The first is that it has often been said that the three most important rules for any witness are "listen, listen, and listen." To respond appropriately and precisely, you must listen to every word of every question with a focus and discipline that none of us use in our normal conversations. The second basic principle sounds even simpler but is actually very hard to achieve. Most witnesses get into difficulty not because they are trying to lie, but rather because they are trying *too hard* to tell the truth. As a result, they end up going beyond what they truly know or remember. So the other principle is simply "don't try too hard." The Ten Rules that follow are really just guides to help you put these two principles into practice.

Grand Jury Testimony (State)

[NB: This describes the Massachusetts procedure. Each state is different.]

You have been subpoenaed to appear as a witness before a state grand jury. This is a very serious proceeding, and it can be a frightening and confusing prospect for most people. This memo is intended to help you understand this process and the difficult but critical job of preparing for your appearance. Please read it carefully, and bring any questions or thoughts that it raises with you when we meet to prepare.

A state grand jury is a group of people, chosen at random, who come together to hear evidence and decide whether there is "probable cause" to believe that someone has committed a crime. The grand jury has broad powers to compel people to testify or produce documents. Witnesses testify under oath, and after hearing testimony and receiving documents, the grand jury may vote on whether or not to bring ("return") formal criminal charges (an "indictment").

The grand jury is an important part of our system of justice, but it is important for a witness to realize that it is neither an open nor an even process. It is not "open" because grand jury proceedings are secret. Only the grand jurors, the prosecutor, the court reporter, and the witnesses are allowed in the room. The witness's counsel may come in but generally cannot say anything or ask any questions (but the witness can go out to talk to counsel as often as desired). Everyone involved—except the witness and his or her counsel—is supposed to keep the proceedings secret.

The grand jury is not "even" because the prosecutor has enormous control over the process. In reality, the prosecutor generally decides who or what the grand jury will investigate, who will appear before them including what witnesses or documents will be subpoenaed, what questions will be asked, and what indictments will be drafted and presented. The prosecutor is under no obligation to present "both sides of the story."

If all this sounds one-sided, it is, and that can make it difficult. Witnesses are not without rights. You have a constitutional right not to incriminate yourself (if you do not already have immunity), an absolute right to consult with counsel at all times, and other rights. However, your most important protection is often careful preparation with counsel. The notion that you can just go in and tell your story in this new and strange environment without intensive preparation is an invitation to disaster.

The oath you will take at the beginning of the grand jury is to tell the truth, the whole truth, and nothing but the truth. Like many things in our normal lives, we tend to blur it all together into one image. Like many things in the precise and artificial world of giving testimony, you need to examine the entire statement and make sure that you understand and seriously consider all three parts. There are, after all, three parts to the oath for good reasons.

In the grand jury, the hardest part of following your oath is to tell nothing but the truth. This takes a surprising amount of preparation, concentration, and internal discipline. Much of what we do or say to keep a normal, casual conversation going must be avoided at a grand jury. In friendly conversation, to avoid looking rude, or foolish, or uninformed, we often embellish or shade our knowledge or understanding in perfectly innocent and acceptable ways. We guess, we assume, we hide our lack of memory or knowledge, we gossip, we talk too much, and we speak without careful thinking. Changing these normal habits is hard work, but it is essential for successful testimony.

Two basic principles should guide you in this effort. The first is that it has often been said that the three most important rules for any witness are "listen, listen, and listen." To respond appropriately and precisely, you must listen to every word of every question with a focus and discipline that none of us use in our normal conversations. The second basic principle sounds even simpler but it is actually very hard to achieve. Most witnesses get into difficulty not because they are trying to lie, but rather because they are trying *too hard* to tell the truth. As a result, they end up going beyond what they truly know or remember. So the other principle is simply "don't try too hard." The Ten Rules that follow are really just guides to help you put these two principles into practice.

Trial

You have been subpoenaed to appear as a witness in a trial. This is a very serious proceeding, and it can be a frightening and confusing prospect for most people. This memo is intended to help you understand this process and the difficult but critical job of preparing for your testimony. Please read it carefully, and bring any questions or thoughts that it raises with you when we meet to prepare.

A trial is a formal proceeding in which the "fact finder" (usually a judge or jury) is presented with evidence (usually testimony of witnesses and documents) and then brings a "verdict" deciding between the side that brought the case (the plaintiff in a civil case, the prosecution in a criminal case) and the defendant. Lawyers represent each side and call and question witnesses. Although the trial is what most people think about when they think of litigation, in fact it is often the culmination of months or even years of investigation, discovery, testimony, legal arguments, and other proceedings. It's important to remember that you are rarely writing on a clean slate.

At a trial, the side that calls a witness to testify questions that witness on direct examination. The opposing side may then question the witness on cross-examination (there may also then be redirect and re-cross). The principal difference involves the use of "leading" questions. These are questions that contain or suggest their own answers (for example, "Isn't it true that it was cold outside?" instead of "What was the weather?"). The purpose of direct examination is for the fact finder to hear what the witness has to say about the matter. Thus, to help make sure that the testimony is that of the witness, not the lawyer, "leading" questions are generally not allowed. Instead, the lawyer will usually ask more open "who, what, when, where, why" types of questions, or follow-ups like "what else" or "what next," and it will be partially up to you to listen, think, and take the initiative to respond fully.

When the other side has a chance to question a witness on cross-examination, everything changes. Their purpose is not to have the witness tell the story again, but for the lawyer to highlight or challenge certain parts, or to challenge the witness's overall credibility. Thus, leading questions are not only allowed, they become the norm. The lawyer will try to do the testifying, and exercise "control" by trying to limit the witness to yes-or-no answers. Of course, the lawyer's words may not accurately reflect what you said, and many questions cannot be answered yes or no. You have to be extraordinarily focused and disciplined to listen carefully and respond clearly and accurately. The notion that you can just go in and tell your story in this new and strange environment without intensive preparation is an invitation to disaster.

The oath you will take at the beginning of your trial testimony is to tell the truth, the whole truth, and nothing but the truth. Like many things in our normal lives, we tend to blur it all together into one image. Like many things in the precise and artificial world of giving testimony, you need to examine the *entire* statement and make sure that you understand and seriously consider all three parts. There are, after all, three parts to the oath for good reasons.

In a trial, the hardest part of following your oath is to tell nothing but the truth. This takes a surprising amount of preparation, concentration, and internal discipline. Much of what we do or say to keep a normal, casual conversation going must be avoided at a trial. In friendly conversation, to avoid looking rude, or foolish, or uninformed, we often embellish or shade our knowledge or understanding in perfectly innocent and acceptable ways. We guess, we assume, we hide our lack of memory or knowledge, we gossip, we talk too much, and we speak without careful thinking. Changing these normal habits is hard work, but it is *essential* for successful testimony.

Two basic principles should guide you in this effort. The first is that it has often been said that the three most important rules for any witness are "listen, listen, and listen." To respond appropriately and precisely, you must listen to every word of every question with a focus and discipline that none of us use in our normal conversations. The second basic principle sounds even simpler, but it is actually very hard to achieve. Most witnesses get into difficulty not because they are trying to lie, but rather because they are trying *too hard* to tell the truth. As a result, they end up going beyond what they truly know or remember. So the other principle is simply "don't try too hard." The Ten Rules that follow are really just guides to help you put these two principles into practice.

Preparation Rules

1. Take Your Time
(Or: He who writes the rules wins the game.)

Follow this rule and the rest will be much easier. There are no shortcuts. The harder you try to move things along and "be helpful," the longer and harder your testimony will be. Instead, right from the *first question*, pause a good five seconds after *every* question before answering. Don't wait until the middle of the testimony to do this; it will be much harder. Remember, it's *your* oath and *your* testimony: *You* should control the pace, whether it makes someone else happy or not. The written record looks the same whether you take a minute or a second to formulate your answer, but your answer will be better for the extra thought. Waiting five seconds after every question will help you in several ways:

(a) It will keep you from feeling rushed. People in a hurry make mistakes. Lawyers know that, and some may try to push you faster just for that reason.

(b) It will give you time to make sure you really understand the question, and to think about the best, most truthful, and most precise answer.

(c) It will give your lawyer time to object, if appropriate. If there is an objection, stop, listen, and wait until you are advised to continue.

2. Always Remember You Are Making a Record

(Or: You can't unring the bell.)

The most important person in the room is the only one who doesn't say anything: the court reporter or other person taking notes. Everything—questions, answers, comments—may be taken down. Answer each question as if you were dictating the first and only draft of an important document (you *are*!). This may help force you to discipline yourself to make a thoughtful, careful reply. Listen to every word of the question; if you are not 100 percent sure of what is being said and asked, be careful!

3. Tell the Truth

(Or: "Always tell the truth: It makes it easier to remember what you said the first time." —Mark Twain)

This is more than a useless maxim; it is a rule of self-preservation. Lying here is not only a crime, it's foolish. Assume that the questioner is more experienced than you think, and that this includes the ability to make a witness who is playing fast and loose with the truth very uncomfortable. Telling the truth includes being yourself, warts and all, without being defensive. It also includes honest mistakes. Witnesses aren't robots; if you make a mistake, just stop and clarify your answer.

4. Be Relentlessly Polite

(Or: Don't tease the bear.)

Everyone here has a job to do. Yours is to listen hard, think carefully, and answer questions if you can. Theirs is to ask questions. Don't waste your time and energy belittling or attacking their job or thinking, saying, or implying negative things about the investigation, the questions, and so on. You will accomplish nothing, you will distract yourself from your difficult job, and you will needlessly antagonize the questioner. If there is a reason for things to get difficult, leave that to your lawyer. Stay above the fray. Don't get angry or defensive; it will only distract you.

5. Don't Answer a Question You Don't Understand

(Or: What we have here is a failure to communicate.)

When you review your transcript, you will be amazed at how many questions were really incomprehensible (or misunderstood). Do not wait until it is too late. You have a right to clear, simple questions, and to answer only questions you understand. Even the best lawyers sometimes phrase questions badly, and even the best witnesses get distracted and don't hear a question. *Don't answer.* Just say, "Would you please rephrase the question." No more than that. Understanding includes being comfortable with a question, the language, and the assumptions that are included. If you're not comfortable with any of these, don't answer the question. Challenge bad assumptions ("Have you stopped beating your spouse?").

6. If You Do Not Remember, Say So

(Or: "I wish I had an answer to that, because I'm tired of answering that question." —Yogi Berra)

The pace of litigation today means that testimony often doesn't happen until months or even years after the events at issue. This is not your fault; it's just reality. Events or facts that may have been insignificant to you even when they happened may now, *much* later, have taken on some significance to the questioner, but you can still testify only to what you precisely remember. This is surprisingly unnatural and difficult. In our normal conversations, we rarely just say "I don't remember," and stop. Rather, we guess and assume to help keep the conversation going (and maybe to make ourselves look smart). *Don't do that in testimony.* If you don't have a clear and precise memory, just say that you don't remember, and stop.

7. Don't Guess

(Or: "If you don't know where you're going, you might wind up somewhere else." —Yogi Berra)

If you are not sure or don't know, say so. Just say, "I don't know," and stop. This, again, is unnatural, but critical. In our everyday conversations, we guess, estimate, and make other kinds of imprecise comments to keep the conversation going, knowing that we will never be cross-examined or held to our precise statement. Everything changes here: You can be only as precise as you are precisely and absolutely certain. "Guessing" includes three broad categories.

Factual Details

It is particularly dangerous to guess about things like dates, times, and numbers. If you say "I don't know," and the questioner pushes for your "best memory," or something like that, make it very clear that "I would have to guess." If he or she still pushes for your best guess, give a range that leaves you a generous margin of error. Don't narrow that wide range unless you're *absolutely* certain.

Inferences

Another type of guessing we also do every day but may not recognize as guessing is the drawing of conclusions, inferences, and opinions. ("Why did X do this?" "What did Y mean by that?") We may know enough about the issue that there's a good chance we're right. That's fine in a normal conversation. In testimony, 95 percent isn't good enough; it must be 100 percent or nothing. That means that you can testify only about what you precisely *saw, heard,* or *did.*

Hypotheticals

Asking you to speculate on what someone could have/would have/should have/must have done, based on limited facts in a lawyer's question, is the worst kind of guessing. Don't guess.

8. Don't Volunteer

(Or: "I never said most of the things I said." —Yogi Berra)

You are there to answer the questions carefully, briefly, and precisely, and then go home. *Keep it simple.* If a question is too long or complex, don't answer it. Ask that it be rephrased. Whatever the question, keep your answer as short, simple, and narrow as possible, and then stop. If a questioner doesn't follow up with more questions, and thereby misses other information, that's not your problem. You should not

- volunteer information beyond the narrow lines of the question;
- help educate the questioner;
- explain your thought processes; or
- fill in the silences.

9. Be Careful with Documents and Prior Statements

(Or: "You can observe a lot, just by watching." —Yogi Berra)

If you are asked a question about a document (or about something that is contained in a document), *ask to see it.* This includes a prior statement or transcript. If you are not allowed to see it, make that clear on the record, and don't guess about what it says. The document will speak for itself. If you *are* allowed to see it, read the *entire* document or statement carefully, as if it were your first time, ask to have the question again, and then focus not just on the words the questioner may have picked out but on the whole portion of the document related to that issue.

10. Use Your Counsel

(Or: "In theory, there's no difference between theory and practice. In practice there is." —Yogi Berra)

Don't be shy about talking to your counsel for whatever reason, and however often. Whatever anyone might say, it doesn't "look bad" on the record, and it will not reflect badly on your testimony. Whether it's because you don't understand a question, aren't comfortable with a new issue, just thought of something, want to review a document, made a mistake, or just need a break, talk to counsel (outside the room, if necessary). Use your counsel in other ways, too:

- Do not agree to supply any information or documents requested by the examiner. Counsel will either answer the request or will take the request under advisement.
- If an objection is made to a question, listen to the objection very carefully. You may learn something about the question and how it could be handled from the objection.

Finally, treat the testimony seriously. Avoid any attempt at levity. Pomposity is the occupational disease of the legal profession. You will be hauled over the coals for not taking your solemn oath seriously if you make jokes or wisecrack. Avoid even the mildest obscenity and avoid absolutely any ethnic or sexual slurs or references that could be considered derogatory. There is no such thing as "off the record." If you have any conversation with anybody other than your counsel, be prepared for questions on that conversation.

Appendix C

How Are Things in Russia?

1. QUESTION: *"How are things in Russia?"*

1. QUESTION: *"How are things in Russia?"*

2. GENERAL:
    —Since when?
    —Compared to what?
    —What part of Russia?

1.   QUESTION: *"How are things in Russia?"*

2.   **GENERAL:**
—Since when?
—Compared to what?
—What part of Russia?

3.   **CATEGORIES:**

Weather
Politics
Economy
Traffic
Museums
Your work
Your family

1.   QUESTION: *"How are things in Russia?"*

2.   **GENERAL:**
    —Since when?
    —Compared to what?
    —What part of Russia?

3.   **CATEGORIES:**   4.   **ANSWERS:**

      Weather   Good
      Politics   Busy
      Economy   Good
      Traffic   Busy
      Museums   Good
      Your work   Busy
      Your family   Good

1. QUESTION: *"How are things in Russia?"*

2. **GENERAL:**
    —Since when?
    —Compared to what?
    —What part of Russia?

3. **CATEGORIES:**   4. **ANSWERS:**

    Weather   Good
    Politics   Busy
    Economy   Good
    Traffic   Busy
    Museums   Good
    Your work   Busy
    Your family   Good

5. **SPECIFIC:**

    Weather
    —What is the temperature in Moscow today?
    —When did it rain last?
    —How hot has it been?
    —Have you heard a forecast for this weekend?

Appendix D

How Was Your Flight?

1. QUESTION: *"How was your flight?"*

1. **QUESTION:** *"How was your flight?"*

2. **GENERAL:** *Which flight? Nonstop from Moscow?*

1. QUESTION: *"How was your flight?"*

2. GENERAL: *Which flight? Nonstop from Moscow?*

3. CATEGORIES:

    Length
    Turbulence
    Book
    Food
    Delays
    Service

1. **QUESTION:** *"How was your flight?"*

2. **GENERAL:** *Which flight? Nonstop from Moscow?*

3. **CATEGORIES:**   4. **ANSWERS:**

   Length   Long
   Turbulence   OK
   Book   Long
   Food   OK
   Delays   Long
   Service   OK

1. QUESTION: *"How was your flight?"*

2. GENERAL: *Which flight? Nonstop from Moscow?*

3. CATEGORIES: 4. ANSWERS:

    Length   Long
    Turbulence   OK
    Book   Long
    Food   OK
    Delays   Long
    Service   OK

5. SPECIFIC:

    Food
    —Did they serve duck?
    —What kind of wine did they serve?
    —Did they give out those hot towels?

How Are Things at the Hospital?

1. QUESTION: *"How are things at the hospital?"*

1.   QUESTION: *"How are things at the hospital?"*

2.   **GENERAL:**
      —Since when?
      —Compared to what?
      —What part of the hospital?

1.   QUESTION: *"How are things at the hospital?"*

2.   **GENERAL:**
     —Since when?
     —Compared to what?
     —What part of the hospital?

3.   **CATEGORIES:**

     ER
     Physical Plant
     HMOs
     Malpractice Suits
     Staff Recruiting
     Bottom Line

1. QUESTION: *"How are things at the hospital?"*

2. GENERAL:
    —Since when?
    —Compared to what?
    —What part of the hospital?

3. CATEGORIES: 4. ANSWERS:

    ER   Good
    Physical Plant   Bad
    HMOs   Good
    Malpractice Suits   Bad
    Staff Recruiting   Good
    Bottom Line   Bad

1. QUESTION: *"How are things at the hospital?"*

2. GENERAL:
    —Since when?
    —Compared to what?
    —What part of the hospital?

3. CATEGORIES:

    ER
    Physical Plant
    HMOs
    Malpractice Suits
    Staff Recruiting
    Bottom Line

4. ANSWERS:

    Good
    Bad
    Good
    Bad
    Good
    Bad

5. SPECIFIC:

    ER
    —What effect have the recent changes in HMOs had on your ER?
    —Are you talking with other ER groups?
    —Has your wait time improved?

Witness Bill of Rights

Witness Bill of Rights

1. You have the right to control the pace of your testimony;
2. You have the right to question the questioner;
3. You have the right to tell your story;
4. You have the right to be treated with respect;
5. You have the right to clear and fair questions;
6. You have the right to forget;
7. You have the right to make clear what you don't know;
8. You have the right to silence.
9. You have the right to see and read all documents;
10. You have the right to use your counsel.

Index

Facts (*continued*)
 in seven steps for witness
   preparation, 51–52
 physician as witness and, 193
 principles of witness
   preparation and, 63
Factual details, guessing about,
  113–114, 211
Faded memory, 109–110
Fairness, 65–66
Fair questions, 61, 95, 96, 97, 103,
  117, 123, 130, 210–211
False declarations before a grand
  jury or court, 6
False statements, 6
Federal Rules of Civil Procedure,
  141, 173, 177, 183, 187,
  206
Fifth Amendment, 159, 159–160,
  197–198
Five Ws, 110
Follow-up question, 56, 104–105
Forms, 127
Four Es, 190
Friend, 16
Frustration
 questioner's, 93
Fundamentals
 memory and, 112

G
Games, 91–92
Gaps
 audience. *See* Audience gap

conversation. *See* Conversation
 gap
perception. *See* Perception gap
witness's real world experiences
 and expectations and, 9
Gates, Bill, 37, 175
Geders v. United States, 202
Goals
 in witness preparation, 25–26
Golden Rule, 117
Grand jury
 defined, 157
 purposes of, 157, 157–158
Grand jury witness
 counsel and, 160–161
 Fifth Amendment and, 159,
  159–160
 immunity and, 159–160
 knowledge and, 162
 overview of, 157–158
 preparation and, 162
 secrecy and, 160–161
 "target" and, 161
 testimony and, 161–162
 the room and, 160
Guessing
 about factual details, 113–114
 about hypotheticals, 117–118
 about inferences, 115–116
 cross-examination and,
  167–168
 danger of, 113–114
 testifying successfully and, 71
 Witness Bill of Rights and, 211
Guide to Taking Testimony in